Back to Basics: Real Estate Investing

by Eric Tyson, MBA, and
Robert S. Griswold, MSBA

Publisher's Acknowledgments

Editorial Project Manager:
Victoria M. Adang

Senior Acquisitions Editor:
Tracy Boggier

Production Editor:
Tamilmani Varadharaj

Cover Images: (magnifying glass)
© AVicons/Getty Images, (house)
© petovarga/Getty Images

Cover Design: Wiley

Back to Basics: Real Estate Investing

Published by John Wiley & Sons, Inc.
111 River St.
Hoboken, NJ 07030-5774
http://www.wiley.com

For general information on our other products and services, please contact our Business Development Department in the U.S. at 317-572-3205.

ISBN 978-1-119-47263-6 (pbk); ISBN 978-1-119-47298-8 (ePub); ISBN 978-1-119-47299-5 (ePDF)

Manufactured in the United States of America

10 9 8 7 6 5 4 3 2 1

Contents

1

Real Estate as an Investment

When Robert first entered the real estate field while attending college decades ago, his father, a retired real estate attorney, advised that he use his monthly income primarily to pay day-to-day living expenses and allocate money each month into long-term financial investments like real estate. This solid advice has served Robert well over the years.

It's never too early or too late to formulate your own plan into a comprehensive wealth-building strategy. For many, such a strategy can help with the challenges of funding future education for children and ensuring a comfortable retirement.

The challenge involved with real estate is that it takes some real planning to get started. Contacting an investment company and purchasing some shares of your favorite mutual fund or stock is a lot easier than acquiring your first rental property. Buying property isn't that difficult, though. You just need a financial and real estate investment plan, a lot of patience, and the willingness to do some hard work, and you're on your way to building your own real estate empire!

In this chapter, we give you some information that can help you decide whether you have what it takes to make money *and* be comfortable with investing in real estate. We compare real estate investments to other investments. We provide some questions you need to ask yourself before making any decisions. Along the way, we share our experience, insights, and thoughts on a long-term strategy for building wealth through real estate that virtually everyone can understand and achieve.

Real Estate's Income- and Wealth-Producing Potential

Compared with most other investments, good real estate can excel at producing periodic or monthly cash flow for property owners. So in addition to the longer-term appreciation potential, you can also earn investment income year in and year out. Real estate is a true growth *and* income investment.

The following list highlights the major benefits of investing in real estate:

- **Tax-deferred compounding of value:** In real estate investing, the appreciation of your properties compounds *tax-deferred* during your years of ownership. You don't pay tax on this profit until you sell your property — and even then you can roll over your gain into another investment property and avoid paying taxes. (See the "Tax advantages" section later in this chapter.)

- **Regular cash flow:** If you have property that you rent out, you have money coming in every month in the form of rents. Some properties, particularly larger multiunit complexes, may have some additional sources, such as from coin-operated washers and dryers.

  When you own investment real estate, you should also expect to incur expenses that include your mortgage payment, property taxes, insurance, and maintenance. The interaction of the revenues coming in and the expenses going out is what tells you whether you realize positive operating profit each month.

- **Reduced income tax bills:** For income tax purposes, you also get to claim an expense that isn't really an out-of-pocket cost — depreciation. Depreciation enables you to reduce your current income tax bill and hence increase your cash flow from a property.

- **Rate of increase of rental income versus overall expenses:** Over time, your operating profit, which is subject to ordinary income tax, should rise as you increase your rental prices faster than the rate of increase for your property's overall expenses. What follows is a simple example to show why even modest rental increases are magnified into larger operating profits and healthy returns on investment over time.

Suppose you're in the market to purchase a single-family home that you want to rent out and that such properties are selling for about $200,000 in the area you've deemed to be a good investment. (*Note:* Housing prices vary widely across different areas, but the following example should give you a relative sense of how a rental property's expenses and revenue change over time.) You expect to make a 20 percent down payment and take out a 30-year fixed-rate mortgage at 6 percent for the remainder of the purchase price — $160,000. Here are the details:

Monthly mortgage payment	$960
Monthly property tax	$200
Other monthly expenses (maintenance, insurance)	$200
Monthly rent	$1,400

In Table 1-1, we show you what happens with your investment over time. We assume that your rent and expenses (except for your mortgage payment, which is fixed) increase 3 percent annually and that your property appreciates a conservative 4 percent per year. (For simplification purposes, we ignore depreciation in this example. If we had included the benefit of depreciation, it would further enhance the calculated returns.)

Year	Monthly Rent	Monthly Expenses	Property Value	Mortgage Balance
0	$1,400	$1,360	$200,000	$160,000
5	$1,623	$1,424	$243,330	$148,960
10	$1,881	$1,498	$296,050	$133,920
20	$2,529	$1,682	$438,225	$86,400
30	$3,398	$1,931	$648,680	$0
31	$3,500	$1,000	$674,625	$0

Table 1-1: *How a Rental Property's Income and Wealth Build Over Time*

Notice what happens over time. When you first buy the property, the monthly rent and the monthly expenses are about equal. By year five, the monthly income exceeds the expenses by about $200 per month. Consider why this happens — your largest monthly expense, the mortgage payment, doesn't increase. So, even though we assume that the rent increases just 3 percent per year, which is the same rate of increase assumed for your nonmortgage expenses, the compounding of rental inflation begins to produce larger and larger cash flow to you, the property owner. Cash flow of $200 per month may not sound like much, but consider that this $2,400 annual income is from an original $40,000 investment. Thus, by year five, your rental property is producing a 6 percent return on your down payment investment. (And if you factor in the tax deduction for depreciation, your cash flow and return are even higher.)

In addition to the monthly cash flow from the amount that the rent exceeds the property's expenses, also look at the last two columns in Table 1-1 to see what has happened by year five to your *equity* (the difference between market value and mortgage balance owed) in the property. With just a 4 percent annual increase in market value, your $40,000 in equity (the down payment) has more than doubled to $94,370 ($243,330 − $148,960).

By years 10 and 20, you can see the further increases in your monthly cash flow and significant expansion in your property's equity. By year 30, the property is producing more than $1,400 per month cash flow, and you're now the proud owner of a mortgage-free property worth more than triple what you paid for it!

After you get the mortgage paid off in year 30, take a look at what happens in year 31 and beyond to your monthly expenses (big drop) and therefore your cash flow (big increase).

Caveats of Real Estate Investing

Despite all its potential, real estate investing isn't lucrative at all times and for all people — here's a quick outline of the biggest caveats that accompany investing in real estate:

- **Few home runs:** Your likely returns from real estate won't approach the home runs that the most accomplished entrepreneurs achieve in the business world.

- **Upfront operating profit challenges:** Unless you make a large down payment, your monthly operating profit may be small, nonexistent, or negative in the early years of rental property ownership. During soft periods in the local economy, rents may rise more slowly than your expenses, or they may even fall. That's why you must ensure that you can weather financially tough times. In the worst cases, we've seen rental property owners lose both their investment property and their homes.

- **Ups and downs:** You're not going to earn an 8 to 10 percent return every year. Although you have the potential for significant profits, owning real estate isn't like owning a printing press at the US Treasury. Like stocks and other types of ownership investments, real estate goes through down as well as up periods. Most people who make money investing in real estate do so because they invest and hold property over many years.

- **Relatively high transaction costs:** If you buy a property and then want out a year or two later, you may find that even though it has appreciated in value, much (if not all) of your profit has been wiped away by the high transaction costs. Typically, the costs of buying and selling — which include real estate agent commissions, loan fees, title insurance, and other closing costs — amount to about 10 to 15 percent of the purchase price of a property. So, although you may be elated if your property appreciates 15 percent in value in short order, you may not be so thrilled to realize that if you sell the property, you may not have any greater return than if you had stashed your money in a bank account.

- **Tax implications:** When you make a positive net return or profit on your real estate investment, the federal and state governments are waiting with open hands for their share. Throughout this book, we highlight ways to improve your after-tax returns. The profit you have left after Uncle Sam takes his bite (not your pretax income) is all that really matters.

These drawbacks shouldn't keep you from exploring real estate investing as an option; rather, they simply reinforce the need to know what you're getting into with this type of investing and whether it's a good match for you. The rest of this chapter takes you deeper into an assessment of real estate as an investment as well as introspection about your goals, interests, and abilities.

Real Estate versus Other Investments

Surely you've considered or heard about many different investments over the years. To help you grasp and understand the unique characteristics of real estate, we compare and contrast real estate's attributes with those of other wealth-building investments like stocks and small business.

Returns

A major reason that many people invest in real estate is for the healthy total *returns* (which include ongoing cash flow and the appreciation of the property). Real estate often generates robust long-term returns because, like stocks and small business, it's an *ownership investment.* By that, we mean that real estate is an asset that has the ability to produce periodic income *and* gain or profits upon refinancing or sale.

Our research and experience suggest that total real estate investment returns are comparable to those from stocks — about 8 to 10 percent annually. Over recent decades, the average annual return on *real estate investment trusts (REITs)* — publicly traded companies that invest in income-producing real estate such as apartment buildings, office complexes, and shopping centers — has appreciated at about this pace as well.

And you can earn long-term returns better than 10 percent per year if you select excellent properties in the best areas, hold them for several years, and manage them well.

Risk

Real estate doesn't always rise in value — witness the decline that occurred in most parts of the United States during the late 2000s. That said, market values for real estate generally don't suffer from as much volatility as stock prices do. You may recall how the excitement surrounding the rapid sustained increase of technology and Internet stock prices in the late 1990s turned into the dismay and agony of those same sectors' stock prices crashing in the early 2000s. Many stocks in this industry saw their stock prices plummet by 80 percent, 90 percent, or more. Generally, you don't see those kinds of dramatic roller-coaster shifts in values over the short run with the residential income property real estate market.

However, keep in mind (especially if you tend to be concerned about shorter-term risks) that real estate can suffer from declines of 10 percent, 20 percent, or more. If you make a down payment of 20 percent and want to sell your property after a 10 to 15 percent price decline, you may find that 100 percent of your invested dollars (down payment) are wiped out after you factor in transaction costs. So you can lose everything.

 You can greatly reduce and minimize your risk investing in real estate through buying and holding property for many years (seven to ten or more).

Liquidity

Liquidity — the ease and cost with which you can sell and get your money out of an investment — is one of real estate's shortcomings. Real estate is relatively *illiquid:* You can't sell a piece of property with the same speed with which you whip out your ATM card and withdraw money from your bank account or sell a stock or a mutual fund with a click of your mouse.

We view real estate's relative illiquidity as a strength, certainly compared with stocks that people often trade in and out of because doing so is so easy and seemingly cheap.

As a result, many stock market investors tend to lose sight of the long term and miss out on the bigger gains that accrue to patient buy-and-stick-with-it investors. Because you can't track the value of investment real estate daily on your computer, and because real estate takes considerable time, energy, and money to sell, you're far more likely to buy and hold onto your properties for the longer term.

Although real estate investments are generally less liquid than stocks, they're generally more liquid than investments made in your own or someone else's small business. People need a place to live and businesses need a place to operate, so there's always demand for real estate (although the supply of such available properties can greatly exceed the demand in some areas during certain time periods).

Capital requirements

Although you can easily get started with traditional investments such as stocks and mutual funds with a few hundred or thousand dollars, the vast majority of quality real estate investments require far greater investments — usually on the order of tens of thousands of dollars.

Diversification value

An advantage of holding investment real estate is that its value doesn't necessarily move in tandem with other investments, such as stocks or small-business investments that you hold. You may recall, for example, the massive stock market decline in the early 2000s. In most communities around America, real estate values were either steady or actually rising during this horrendous period for stock prices.

However, real estate prices and stock prices, for example, *can* move down together in value (witness the severe recession and stock market drop that took hold in 2008). Sluggish business conditions and lower corporate profits can depress stock *and* real estate prices.

Opportunities to add value

Although you may not know much about investing in the stock market, you may have some good ideas about how to improve a property and make it more valuable. You can fix up a property or develop it further and raise the rental income accordingly. Perhaps through legwork, persistence, and good negotiating skills, you can purchase a property below its fair market value.

_____

_____

_____

Relative to investing in the stock market, tenacious and savvy real estate investors can more easily buy property in the private real estate market at below fair market value because the real estate market is somewhat less efficient and some owners don't realize the value of their income property or they need to sell quickly. Theoretically, you can do the same in the stock market, but the scores of professional, full-time money managers who analyze the public market for stocks make finding bargains more difficult.

Tax advantages

Real estate investment offers numerous tax advantages. In this section, we compare and contrast investment property tax issues with those of other investments.

Deductible expenses (including depreciation)

Owning a property has much in common with owning your own small business. Every year, you account for your income and expenses on a tax return. For now, we want to remind you to keep good records of your expenses in purchasing and operating rental real estate. One expense that you get to deduct for rental real estate on your tax return — depreciation — doesn't involve spending money. *Depreciation* is an allowable tax deduction for buildings, because structures wear out over time. Under current tax laws, residential real estate is depreciated over 27½ years (commercial buildings are less favored in the tax code and can be depreciated over 39 years). Residential real estate is depreciated over shorter time periods because it has traditionally been a favored investment in US tax laws.

Tax-free rollovers of rental property profits

When you sell a stock, mutual fund, or exchange-traded investment that you hold outside a retirement account, you must pay tax on your profits. By contrast, you can avoid paying tax on your profit when you sell a rental property if you roll over your gain into a like-kind investment real estate property.

The rules for properly making one of these 1031 exchanges are complex and involve third parties. Make sure you find an attorney and/or tax advisor who is an expert at these transactions to ensure you meet the technical and strict timing requirements so everything goes smoothly (and legally).

If you don't roll over your gain, you may owe significant taxes because of how the IRS defines your gain. For example, if you buy a property for $200,000 and sell it for $550,000, you not only owe tax on the gain from the increased property value, but you also owe tax on an additional amount, the property's depreciation you used during your ownership. The amount of depreciation that you deduct on your tax returns reduces the original $200,000 purchase price, making the taxable difference that much larger. For example, if you deducted $125,000 for depreciation over the years that you owned the property, you owe tax on the difference between the sale price of $550,000 and $75,000 ($200,000 purchase price – $125,000 depreciation).

Determining Whether You Should Invest in Real Estate

Most people can succeed at investing in real estate if they're willing to do their homework, which includes selecting top real estate professionals. In the sections that follow, we ask several important questions to help you decide whether you have what it takes to succeed and be happy with real estate investments that involve managing property. Income-producing real estate isn't a passive investment.

Do you have sufficient time?

Purchasing and owning investment real estate and being a landlord is time-consuming. The same way an uninformed owner can sell his property for less than it's worth, if you fail to do your homework before purchasing property, you can end up overpaying or buying real estate with a slew of problems. Finding competent and ethical real estate professionals takes time (see Chapter 3). Investigating communities, neighborhoods, and zoning also soaks up plenty of hours, as does examining tenant issues with potential properties.

As for managing a property, you can hire a property manager to interview tenants, collect the rent, and solve problems such as leaky faucets and broken appliances, but doing so costs money and still requires some of your time.

Can you deal with problems?

Challenges and problems inevitably occur when you try to buy a property. Purchase negotiations can be stressful and frustrating. You can also count on some problems coming up when you own and manage investment real estate. Most tenants won't care for a property the way property owners do.

_____

_____

_____

If every little problem (especially those that you think may have been caused by your tenants) causes you distress, at a minimum, you should only own rental property with the assistance of a property manager. You should also question whether you're really going to be happy owning investment property. The financial rewards come well down the road, but you live the day-to-day ownership headaches immediately.

Does real estate interest you?

Some of the best real estate investors have a curiosity and interest in real estate. If you don't already possess it, such an interest and curiosity *can* be cultivated.

On the other hand, some people simply aren't comfortable investing in rental property. For example, if you've had experience and success with stock market investing, you may be uncomfortable venturing into real estate investments. Some people are on a mission to start their own business and may prefer to channel the time and money into that outlet.

Can you handle market downturns?

Real estate investing isn't for the faint of heart. Buying and holding real estate is a whole lot of fun when prices and rents are rising. But market downturns happen, and they test you emotionally as well as financially.

Consider the real estate market price declines that happened in most communities and types of property in the late 2000s. Such drops can present attractive buying opportunities for those with courage and cash.

None of us has a crystal ball though, so don't expect to be able to buy at the precise bottom of prices and sell at the exact peak of your local market. Even if you make a smart buy now, you'll inevitably end up holding some of your investment property during a difficult market. Do you have the financial wherewithal to handle such a downturn? How have you handled other investments when their values have fallen?

_____

_____

_____

2

Common Real Estate Investments

If you lack substantial experience investing in real estate, we advise that you begin with more accessible and easy-to-master income-producing property options, which we discuss in this chapter. In particular, *residential income property* can be an attractive real estate investment for many people. Residential housing is easier to understand, purchase, and manage than most other types of property, such as office, industrial, and retail property. If you're a homeowner, you already have experience locating, purchasing, and maintaining residential property.

Residential Income Property

The first (and one of the best) real estate investments for many people is a home in which to live. In this section, we cover the investment possibilities inherent in buying a home for your own use, including potential profit to be had from converting your home to a rental or fixing it up and selling it. We also give you some pointers on how to profit from owning your own vacation home.

A place of your own

During your adult life, you're going to need a roof over your head for many decades. And real estate is the only investment that you can live in or rent out to produce income.

Unless you expect to move within the next few years, buying a place may make good long-term financial sense. (Even if you need to relocate, you may decide to continue owning the property and use it as a rental property.) Owning usually costs less than renting over the long term and allows you to build *equity* (the difference between market value and the current balance of the mortgage against the property) in an asset.

_____

_____

_____

Under current tax law, you can also pocket substantial tax-free profits when you sell your home for more than you originally paid plus the money you sunk into improvements during your ownership. Specifically, single taxpayers can realize up to a $250,000 tax-free capital gain; married couples filing jointly get up to $500,000. To qualify for this home-owner's *gains tax exemption,* you (or your spouse if you're married) must have owned the home and used it as your primary residence for a minimum of 24 months out of the past 60 months. The 24 months doesn't have to be continuous. Additionally, the IRS now provides for pro-rata (proportionate) credit based on hardship or change of employment. Also note that the full exemption amounts are reduced proportionately for the length of time you rented out your home over the five-year period referenced above.

Some commentators have stated that your home isn't an investment because you're not renting it out. We respectfully disagree: Consider the fact that many people move to a less costly home when they retire (because it's smaller and/ or because it's in a lower cost area). Trading down to a lower priced property in retirement frees up equity that has built up over many years of homeownership. This money can be used to supplement your retirement income and for many other purposes. Your home is an investment because it can appreciate in value over the years, and you can use that money toward your financial or personal goals. The most recent version of *Home Buying Kit For Dummies* (Wiley), which Eric co-wrote with residential real estate expert Ray Brown, can help you make terrific home buying decisions.

Converting your home to a rental

Turning your current home into a rental property when you move is a simple way to buy and own more properties. You can do this multiple times (as you move out of homes you own over the years), and you can execute this strategy of acquiring rental properties not only with a house, but also with a duplex or other small rental property where you reside in one of the units. This approach is an option if you're already considering investing in real estate, and you can afford to own two or more properties. Holding onto your current home when you're buying a new one is more advisable if you're moving within the same area so you're close by to manage the property. This approach presents several positives:

- You save the time and cost of finding a separate rental property, not to mention the associated transaction costs.

- You know the property and have probably taken good care of it and perhaps made some improvements.

- You know the target market because the home appealed to you.

Some people make the mistake of holding onto their current home for the wrong reasons when they buy another. This situation often happens when a homeowner must sell his home in a depressed market. Nobody likes to lose money and sell their home for less than they paid for it. Thus, some owners hold onto their homes until prices recover. If you plan to move and want to keep your current home as a long-term investment (rental) property, you can. If you fully convert your home to rental property and use it that way for years before selling it, when you do sell, you can either take advantage of the lower long-term capital gains rates or do a tax-deferred exchange. For tax purposes, you get to deduct depreciation and all of the write-offs during the ownership, and you can shelter up to $25,000 in income from active sources subject to income eligibility requirements.

_____

_____

_____

Turning your home into a *short-term* rental, however, is usually a bad move because:

- You may not want the responsibilities of being a landlord, yet you force yourself into the landlord business when you convert your home into a rental.

- You owe tax on the sale's profit if your property is classified for tax purposes as a rental when you sell it and don't buy another rental property. (You can purchase another rental property through a 1031 exchange to defer paying taxes on your profit.)

You lose some of the capital gains tax exclusion if you sell your home and you had rented it out for a portion of the five-year period before selling it. For example, if you rented your home for two of the last five years, you may only exclude 60 percent of your gain (up to the maximums of $250,000 for single taxpayers and $500,000 for married couples filing jointly), whereas the other 40 percent is taxed as a long-term capital gain. Also be aware that when you sell a home previously rented and are accounting for the sale on your tax return, you have to recapture the depreciation taken during the rental period.

Investing and living in fixer-uppers

Serial home selling is a variation on the tried-and-true real estate investment strategy of investing in well-located fixer-upper homes where you can invest your time, sweat equity, and materials to make improvements that add more value than they cost. The only catch is that you must move into the fixer-upper for at least 24 months to earn the full home-owner's capital gains exemption of up to $250,000 for single taxpayers and $500,000 for married couples filing jointly (as we cover in the "A place of your own" section earlier in this chapter).

 Be sure to buy a home in need of TLC in a great neighborhood where you're willing to live for 24 months or more.

Here's a simple example to illustrate the potentially significant benefits of this strategy. You purchase a fixer-upper for $275,000 that becomes your principal residence, and then over the next 24 months you invest $25,000 in improvements (paint, repairs, landscaping, appliances, decorator items, and so on), and you also invest the amount of sweat equity that suits your skills and wallet. You now have one of the nicer homes in the neighborhood, and you can sell this home for a net price of $400,000 after your transaction costs. With your total investment of $300,000 ($275,000 plus $25,000), your efforts have earned you a $100,000 profit completely tax-free. Thus, you've earned an average of $50,000 per year, which isn't bad for a tax-exempt second income without strict office hours. (Note that many states also allow you to avoid state income taxes on the sale of your personal residence, using many of the same requirements as the federal tax laws.)

Now, some cautions are in order here. This strategy is clearly not for everyone interested in making money from real estate investments. We recommend that you bypass this strategy if any of the following apply:

- You're unwilling or reluctant to live through redecorating, minor remodeling, or major construction.
- You dislike having to move every few years.
- You're not experienced or comfortable with identifying undervalued property and improving it.
- You lack a financial cushion to withstand a significant downturn in your local real estate market.

- You don't have the budget to hire a professional contractor to do the work, and you don't have the free time or the home improvement skills needed to enhance the value of a home.

One final caution: Beware of transaction costs. The expenses involved with buying and selling property — such as real estate agent commissions, loan fees, title insurance, and so forth — can consume a large portion of your profits. With most properties, the long-term appreciation is what drives your returns. Consider keeping homes you buy and improve as long-term investment properties.

Vacation homes

Many people of means expand their real estate holdings by purchasing a *vacation home* — a home in an area where they enjoy taking pleasure trips. For most people, buying a vacation home is more of a consumption decision than an investment decision. That's not to say you can't make a profit from owning a second home. However, potential investment returns shouldn't be the main reason you buy a second home.

The advantage of owning a vacation home is that you no longer have to secure accommodations when you want to enjoy some downtime in your ideal vacation destination. Also, when you arrive at your home away from home, you're home!

The downsides to vacation homes can be numerous, including

- **Expenses:** With a second home, you have nearly all the costs of a primary home — mortgage interest, property taxes, insurance, repairs and maintenance, utilities, and so on.

- **Property management:** When you're not at your vacation home, things can go wrong. A pipe can burst, for example, and the mess may not be found for days or weeks. Unless the property is close to a good neighbor or other kind person willing to keep an eye on it for you, you may incur the additional expense of paying a property manager to watch the property for you.

- **Lack of rental income:** Most people don't rent out their vacation homes, thus negating the investment property income stream that contributes to the returns real estate investors enjoy (see Chapter 1). If your second home is in a vacation area where you have access to plenty of short-term renters, you or your designated property manager can rent out the property. However, this entails all of the headaches and hassles of having many short-term renters. (But you gain the tax advantages of depreciation and all expenses as with other rental properties.)

- **Obligation to use:** Some second homeowners complain about feeling forced to use their vacation homes.

Before you buy a second home, weigh all the pros and cons. If you have a spouse or partner with whom you're buying the property, have a candid discussion. Also consult with your tax advisor for other tax-saving strategies for your second home or vacation home.

Types of Residential Properties

If you've been in the market for a home, you know that in addition to single-family homes, you can choose from numerous types of attached or shared housing including duplexes, triplexes, apartment buildings, condominiums, and townhomes. In this section, we provide an overview of each of these properties and show how they may make an attractive real estate investment for you.

From an investment perspective, our top recommendations are apartment buildings and single-family homes. We generally don't recommend attached-housing units. If you can afford a smaller single-family home or apartment building rather than a shared-housing unit, buy the single-family home or apartments.

Unless you can afford a large down payment (25 percent or more), the early years of rental property ownership may financially challenge you: With all properties, as time goes on, generating a positive cash flow gets easier because your mortgage expense stays fixed (if you use fixed-rate financing) while your rents increase faster than your expenses. Regardless of what you choose to buy, make sure you run the numbers on your rental income and expenses (see Chapter 8) to see if you can afford the negative cash flow that often occurs in the early years of ownership.

Single-family homes

As an investment, single-family detached homes generally perform better in the long run than attached or shared housing.

In a good real estate market, most housing appreciates, but single-family homes tend to outperform other housing types for the following reasons:

- Single-family homes tend to attract more potential buyers — most people, when they can afford it, prefer a detached or stand-alone home, especially for the increased privacy.

- Attached or shared housing is less expensive and easier to build *and overbuild;* because of this surplus potential, such property tends to appreciate more moderately in price.

Because so many people prefer to live in detached, single-family homes, market prices for such dwellings can often become inflated beyond what's justified by the rental income these homes can produce. To discover whether you're buying in such a market, compare the monthly cost (after tax) of owning a home to monthly rent for that same property. Focus on markets where the rent exceeds or comes close to equaling the cost of owning and shun areas where the ownership costs exceed rents.

Single-family homes that require just one tenant are simpler to deal with than a multiunit apartment building that requires the management and maintenance of multiple renters and units. The downside, though, is that a vacancy means you have no income coming in. Look at the effect of 0 percent occupancy for a couple of months on your projected income-and-expense statement! By contrast, one vacancy in a four-unit apartment building (each with the same rents) means you're still taking in 75 percent of the gross potential (maximum total) rent.

With a single-family home, you're responsible for all repairs and maintenance. You can hire someone to do the work, but you still have to find the contractors and coordinate and oversee the work. Also recognize that if you purchase a single-family home with many fine features and amenities, you may find it more stressful and difficult to have tenants living in your property who don't treat it with the same care that you may.

The first rule of being a successful landlord is to let go of any emotional attachment to a home. But that sort of attachment on the tenant's part is favorable: The more they make your rental property their home, the more likely they are to stay and return it to you in good condition — except for the expected normal wear and tear of day-to-day living.

Making a profit in the early years of ownership from the monthly cash flow with a single-family home is generally the hardest stage. The reason: Such properties usually sell at a premium price relative to the rent that they can command (you pay extra for the land, which you can't rent). Also remember that with just one tenant, you have no rental income when you have a vacancy.

Attached housing

As the cost of land has climbed over the decades in many areas, packing more housing units that are attached into a given plot of land keeps housing somewhat more affordable. Shared housing makes more sense for investors who don't want to deal with building maintenance and security issues.

In this section, we discuss the investment merits of two forms of attached housing: condominiums and townhomes.

Condos

Condominiums are typically apartment-style units stacked on top of and/or beside one another and sold to individual owners. When you purchase a condominium, you're actually purchasing the interior of a specific unit as well as a proportionate interest in the common areas — the pool, tennis courts, grounds, hallways, laundry room, and so on. Although you (and your tenants) have full use and enjoyment of the common areas, the homeowner's association actually owns and maintains the common areas as well as the building structures themselves (which typically include the foundation, exterior walls, roof, plumbing, electrical, and other major building systems).

One advantage to a condo as an investment property is that of all the attached housing options, condos are generally the lowest-maintenance properties because most condominium or homeowner associations deal with issues such as roofing, landscaping, and so on, for the entire building. Note that you're still responsible for necessary maintenance inside your unit, such as servicing appliances, floor and window coverings, interior painting, and so on.

Although condos may be somewhat easier to keep up, they tend to appreciate less than single-family homes or apartment buildings unless the condo is located in a desirable urban area.

Townhomes

Townhomes are essentially attached or row homes — a hybrid between a typical airspace-only condominium and a single-family house. Like condominiums, townhomes are generally attached, typically sharing walls and a continuous roof. But townhomes are often two-story buildings that come with a small yard and offer more privacy than a condominium because you don't have someone living on top of your unit.

As with condominiums, you must review the governing documents before you purchase the property to see exactly what you legally own. The common areas are part of a larger single lot, and each owner holds title to a proportionate share of the common area.

Apartments

Not only do apartment buildings generally enjoy healthy long-term appreciation potential, but they also often produce positive *cash flow* (rental income – expenses) in the early years of ownership. But as with a single-family home, the buck stops with you for maintenance of an apartment building. You may hire a property manager to assist you, but you still have oversight responsibilities (and additional expenses).

_____

_____

_____

In the real-estate financing world, apartment buildings are divided into two groups based on the number of units:

- **Four or fewer units:** You can obtain more favorable financing options and terms for apartment buildings that have four or fewer units because they're treated as residential property.

- **Five or more units:** Complexes with five or more units are treated as commercial property and don't enjoy the extremely favorable loan terms of the one- to four-unit properties.

Apartment buildings, particularly those with more units, generally produce a small positive cash flow, even in the early years of rental ownership.

3

Your Real Estate Team

For most real estate investors, real estate investing is hands-on and complicated enough to require the services and knowledge of a team of professionals. Although you may be skilled in your chosen field, it's unlikely that you possess all of the varied and detailed skills and knowledge necessary to initiate and close a good real estate transaction.

Evaluate proposed real estate investments carefully and methodically before you make the ultimate purchase decision. The uniqueness of each potential real estate opportunity requires the investor to critique the pending investment. You should understand the economic climate and potential for growth, the current physical condition of the property, the tenants, and the value of the property in the marketplace. Then you should ensure that you've got a solid negotiating strategy to orchestrate a deal, that the financing comes through, and that the transfer of real estate is handled properly. This requires a team approach.

In this chapter, we discuss the different real estate professionals and service providers whom you should consider teaming up with as you search for real estate investment opportunities and proceed with the purchase of property.

When to Establish Your Team

Some real estate investors make the mistake of looking for a property to buy without spending enough time upfront identifying the pros whose help should be retained. We recommend that you have your team in place before you begin your serious property searching for two reasons:

- **You can move quickly.** The speed at which you can close a transaction is an advantage in any type of market. In a soft or buyer's market, some sellers are desperate for cash and need to close quickly. In a rising or seller's market, sellers typically don't tolerate having their property tied up for a long time until closing with a buyer who doesn't understand the current market conditions or how to properly evaluate the property.

- **You can effectively research the property before making an offer.** Prudent investors conduct research and gather information before they make an offer so they know which property is worth seriously pursuing. Typically, the real estate industry describes *due diligence* as the period of time after you place a property under contract (see Chapter 10). But you need to perform due diligence before making an offer. You don't want to waste time or money on a property that can't meet your goals.

Only make an offer when you have done enough due diligence to feel comfortable that your further, thorough review of the property interiors and books probably won't reveal any surprises that will lead to canceling the purchase.

The most effective research is done with the assistance of real estate professionals to give you the advice and information you need to make an intelligent decision. This pre-offer period is critical; it's the one real opportunity for a prospective buyer to investigate a property while retaining the ability to terminate the transaction without a significant monetary loss.

Tax Advisor

A tax advisor may not be the first person that you think to consult before making a real estate transaction. However, our experience is that a good tax advisor can highlight potential benefits and pitfalls of different real estate investment strategies. Of course, make sure your tax person has experience with real estate investing and understands your needs and specific goals in regard to your property investments.

Although you may pick up a lot of information about real estate and discover some of the advantages of property investing by speaking with some tax people, don't rely on generic information. You need specific feedback and ideas from a tax expert regarding your unique financial situation and which types of real estate investments work best for you.

Based on your age, income, and other important factors, the benefits you seek from real estate may be entirely different from other investors. Many real estate investors are looking for immediate cash flow from their properties. But others have sufficient income from other sources and prefer to look at real estate as a wealth builder for their retirement years. And almost all real estate investors are looking for tax benefits.

The role of your accountant is to evaluate and recommend investments and tax strategies that maximize your financial position. Meet with your tax advisor and get to know the benefits and pitfalls of your proposed real estate investments before you start making offers.

Mortgage Broker or Lender

Before looking at specific real estate opportunities, you need a budget. And because your budget for real estate purchases is largely a function of how much you can borrow (in addition to your cash available for a down payment), you need to determine the limits on your borrowing power. If you can't afford a property, it doesn't matter how great a deal it is.

Postpone making an appointment to look at investment properties until after you examine the loans available. You have two resources to consult:

- **Lender** is a generic term for any firm, public or private, that directly loans you the cash you need to purchase your property. This type of lender is often referred to as a *direct lender*. Most often, your list of possible lenders includes banks, credit unions, and private lenders. Lenders tend to specialize in certain types of loans.

- A **mortgage broker** is a service provider that presents your request for a loan to a variety of different lenders to find the best financing for your particular needs. Just like real estate or insurance brokers, a good mortgage broker can be a real asset to your team.

Lending nuances

Lenders and mortgage brokers are in the business of making loans. That's how they make money. Their product is cash, and they make money by renting it to people and businesses that pay back the money plus *interest*, which is the cost of renting the money.

_____

_____

_____

Lenders and mortgage brokers want to find you money for your next real estate purchase, but they're not objective advisors to provide counsel regarding how much you should borrow. They're trained to calculate the maximum that you *may* borrow. Don't confuse this figure with the amount that you *can afford* or that fits best with your overall financial and personal situation. Because they are paid only when they make loans, some lenders and brokers are willing to make any loan.

So why is getting a loan so difficult at times? Because lenders want to make loans to those investors who are a good credit risk and who they think have a high probability of repaying the loan in full plus the interest. The lender has costs of doing business and needs to make a profit. Because the money they lend often belongs to their depositors, lenders need to be careful and selective about the loans they make.

On the upside, lenders can also serve a valuable role by preventing you from making serious mistakes. Particularly in overheated sellers' markets where prices are climbing with little fundamental economic support, your lender and the required appraisal from a competent professional appraiser can keep you from getting caught up in a buy-at-any-price frenzy. In these markets, lenders tend to be a little more conservative, limiting loan amounts and requiring larger down payments.

The lender requires collateral for protection if the borrower doesn't make the debt service payments as required. *Collateral* is the real or personal property that's pledged to secure a loan or mortgage. If the debt isn't paid as agreed, the lender has the right to force the sale of the collateral to recover the outstanding principal and interest on the loan. Typically, the property being purchased is the pledged collateral for real estate loans or mortgages.

Building relationships with lenders

Relationships with lenders can take time to build, so begin looking for lenders that specialize in the types of properties within the geographic area you've targeted. They can help you understand your financial qualifications or how much you can borrow before you begin your search for an investment property. Although lenders only make money by making loans, the type of lender you should associate with is one who understands real estate cycles and your local real estate market.

When you get together with your lender or mortgage broker, provide your latest personal financial statement, which includes your income and expenses as well as your assets and liabilities and net worth.

Always be truthful with your lender. One way to sabotage a relationship with a lender is to exaggerate or stretch the truth about your current financial situation or about the potential for your proposed property acquisition. Most lenders require supporting documents for your income and assets and will obtain a current credit report.

Real Estate Broker or Agent

Your investment team should include a sharp and energetic real estate broker or agent. All real estate brokers and agents are licensed by the state in which they perform their services. A real estate *broker* is the highest level of licensed real estate professional; a licensed real estate sales *agent* is qualified to handle real estate listings and transactions under the supervision of a broker. The vast majority of real estate licensees are sales agents. Throughout this chapter, we refer to both real estate brokers and agents simply as agents.

A real estate agent must have his license placed under a supervising broker who's ultimately responsible for the actions of their sales agents. Real estate brokers often begin their careers as real estate agents. Brokers and agents can perform the same functions; many real estate agents actually have more practical experience and hands-on market knowledge than the brokers they work for. Brokers who have many agents reporting to them often spend most of their time educating, supervising, and reviewing the transactions presented by their agents. If you have a problem with an agent, contact the broker.

 Generally, you deal with real estate agents, but the added experience and dedication of a broker can be beneficial to you if you're involved in larger and/or more complicated transactions.

Whether you use a broker or an agent, make sure the person has a solid track record with investment property transactions in your area.

The value of working with an agent

In many metropolitan areas, looking at the properties on a Multiple Listing Service (MLS) or in online listings isn't enough. The best deals are often the ones that don't make it into these sources. This is where the "insider information" from real estate sales agents can work to your advantage.

You want to be the first one contacted about the best properties coming on the market rather than one of many when everyone knows about the property from the MLS. The *MLS* is a service created and maintained by real estate professionals per guidelines established by the National Association of Realtors (NAR). This service gathers all of the local property listings into a single place so purchasers can review all available properties from one source. The MLS also deals with commission splitting and other relations between agents.

Several investment real estate listing services offer instant access to an incredible database of information on all types of properties. Two of the most popular listing services for investment properties are Loopnet (www.loopnet.com) and CoStar (www.costar.com).

Who the agent works for

When you deal with a real estate agent, you need to know who she represents. Real estate investors need to understand the concepts of dual agency and single agency and the implications of each:

- **Single agency:** This is when an agent represents only the buyer or the seller. The other party either represents herself or is represented by an agent who doesn't work for the same broker as the other agent. For example, a buyer's agent only has a fiduciary relationship with the buyer. The buyer's agent has a duty to promote the interests of the buyer and keep all information confidential unless legally required to disclose. The buyer's interest should be first and foremost, and no information is passed to the seller without your knowledge other than that information that directly affects your ability to perform on the contract as written.

We strongly recommend that you work with an agent who operates as a single agency representative. A lot of money is involved in income property transactions, and you want to have someone looking out for your interests whether you're buying or selling an investment property.

- **Dual agency:** A situation in which the same individual agent represents both the seller and the buyer *or* when two different agents representing the seller and buyer are from the same firm (with the same broker). With any transaction, each agent involved owes a fiduciary duty of loyalty to each client he represents, but this is nearly impossible for one agent who is representing both the buyer and seller in the same transaction.

Avoid the inherent conflict of interest found with dual agency and establish a relationship with a single agency agent who represents only *your* interests.

Agent compensation

Real estate agents are motivated to see the transaction go through because they're compensated when a sale is made. Compensation for agents is typically calculated as a percentage of the sales price paid for a property. So the agents have an interest in the property going for a higher price. Commissions vary based on the property and the size of the transaction:

- Individual residential properties, such as single-family homes and condos, have commissions of 5 to 6 percent of the sales price.

- Small multifamily and commercial properties are often in the 3 to 5 percent range.

- Larger investment properties have commissions of 1 to 3 percent.

These commissions are typically split between the firm listing the property for sale and working with the seller and the agent representing the buyer. The actual proportion of the split varies, with the listing agent sometimes taking a smaller percentage than the buyer's agent if the commissions aren't evenly split. The commission is paid to the broker, and the agent receives his share based on his employment or commission agreement, which also often calls for the agent to cover some of his own expenses and overhead.

Real estate commissions can be a significant cost factor for real estate investors. Most listing agreements acknowledge that commissions aren't fixed by law and are negotiable. Traditionally, the seller "pays" the commission to the real estate agents involved in the transaction, although because the buyer is the one paying for the property, both the buyer and seller ultimately pay for the agent's commissions.

Real estate agents do add to the cost of purchasing property, but a good agent, like a good property manager, can justify the cost of her services by introducing you to properties that you wouldn't otherwise have an opportunity to purchase. A good agent earns her commissions other ways as well — as a good negotiator and through her other marketplace knowledge.

Finding a good broker or agent

The key to finding a good broker or agent to assist you in the purchase of investment real estate is to narrow the field down to those individuals who are the best. Look for folks with the following qualifications:

- **Full-time professional:** Because the commissions earned on the sale of a large income property can be so great, almost every broker or agent will claim that she can represent you. But you want to eliminate those brokers or agents who are greedy, incompetent, or simply mediocre. Although many part-time real estate professionals sell single-family homes and condos, you'll quickly find that the most qualified real estate investment property agents are full time.

- **Expert in the geographic market and specific property type:** Find someone who knows your market and the specific property type you're seeking. This knowledge is especially important if you don't live nearby. Avoid brokers who aren't experts in your specific property type.

_____

_____

_____

Some real estate investment books advise you to contact every broker or real estate agent who targets your preferred geographic area. Although casting a bigger net has some inherent attraction, our experience is that you should only work with one broker or agent at a time in a given market area.

Real estate agents can be a key source for new investment opportunities and general market information. This is where finding an experienced agent who specializes in the types of properties you're looking for and knows the local market pays off. These agents know buyers and sellers and also possess contacts for other services and products that you need as your real estate investment portfolio expands.

After narrowing down the candidates, you can apply standard screening techniques to pinpoint the top three to interview:

- **Verify the professional's license status:** Nearly every state has an online broker and agent database, so this step is simple. Confirm that the professional's real estate license is current with no citations or disciplinary action for past or pending violations. Note that not all states will post pending violations but only adjudicated or resolved matters, so ask your agent directly. If you're using a real estate agent, check both the license status of the agent and her supervising broker. If the broker or agent has been disciplined by the state, inquire further to understand the relevance to your transaction. A suspension or temporary revocation of a license can be a serious issue — even if it was reinstated. The facts of the case may be material to your choice of a real estate professional.

- **Check references:** Get the names and numbers for at least three clients (in the geographical area where you're seeking property) that the broker or agent has worked with in the past year. Investment real estate transactions tend to be fewer than owner-occupied property transactions, so speaking with three or more clients from the last year maximizes your chances of speaking with clients other than the agent's all-time favorites.

Don't just ask for the references; call them. And don't just ask generic questions about whether the client was happy with the broker or agent. Dig deeper — find an agent who you can work with on investments that are critical to your long-term wealth-building goals.

_____

_____

_____

Ask questions about the types of properties and the geographic locations involved. Ask questions like, "Did the broker or agent assertively represent you and take charge of the transaction or did you have to initiate conversations?"

Consider these traits when investigating potential brokers and agents as well:

- **Willingness to communicate with you:** The number one complaint about real estate professionals is that they don't keep their clients informed during transactions. You're looking for someone with experience who isn't necessarily the top producer because you want someone who can take the time to communicate regularly with you.

- **Interpersonal skills:** An agent needs to get along with you and with a whole host of others involved in a typical real estate deal: other agents, property sellers, inspectors, lenders, and so on. An agent needs to know how to put your interests first without upsetting others.

- **Negotiation skills:** Putting a real estate deal together involves negotiation, so you want a broker or agent with negotiating skills and lots of experience in larger transactions. Is your agent going to exhaust all avenues to get you the best deal possible? Be sure to ask the agent's former clients how the agent negotiated for them.

- **Reputation for honesty, integrity, and patience:** When it comes to the brokering of investment properties, the reputation of your representative can be critical. Brokers or agents with a track record of dealing fairly with their clients and their peers can greatly assist in gaining the cooperation of an adversarial seller. And gaining such cooperation is often needed to close a complicated transaction. Some strife is almost guaranteed when buying investment real estate — there are several opportunities where the transaction can unravel, and only the trustworthiness, perseverance, and patience of the real estate professionals involved can keep the transaction on course.

Working with your agent

To get the best deals, timing is critical. You want your broker or agent to think of you first. To do this, you need to build a solid rapport with your agent, which you can do by building a track record of not wasting the time of your professional team.

_____

_____

_____

Because agents only get paid for deals they close, they're not interested in investing time and energy with numerous potential buyers. They want serious buyers who will close the deal. Plus, if you garner a reputation of tying up properties and then renegotiating the deal or canceling the escrow, you'll find that your offers won't be accepted in the future. Sellers and their brokers don't want to waste time with phantom buyers.

Appraiser

Many real estate investors know appraisers solely in the role of providing the property valuation report required by lenders. And it's generally in this role that investors can find appraisers to be a source of aggravation rather than a potential resource. However, an appraiser can be an effective team member if your real estate investment strategy involves buying and selling properties with somewhat-hidden opportunities to add value. Appraisers see many properties over their career and often possess insight into real estate opportunities that others miss.

Appraisers can help you by telling you the current value of a property, but they bring real value as part of your real estate investment team by

- Providing insight into the factors that can lead to an increase in the market value of a property.

- Assisting you in maximizing the return on your investment by suggesting cost-effective and high demand upgrades to distressed or fixer-upper properties.

- Giving you useful information on the demographics of the area and helping to identify those properties that are distressed but have plenty of upside potential (properties requiring work in good neighborhoods).

TIP

Appraisals are often an art and can be very subjective. You need to make sure you find an appraiser who has a comprehensive education and training in proper appraisal techniques and complies with the Uniform Standards of Professional Appraisal Practice (USPAP) set out by the Appraisal Foundation. The appraiser you use should have extensive product knowledge of your target property type (residential, commercial, and so on) along with significant experience and market knowledge in your area. Contact the local American Society of Appraisers and the Appraisal Institute for referrals.

4

Sources of Capital

For many people, the trouble with real estate investing is that they lack the access to cash for the down payment. The old adage that "it takes money to make money" is generally true. Most real estate investing books make one of two assumptions. Some assume you have plenty of money and just need to figure out how to buy, add value to a property, and then sell. The other common assumption is that you have no money and must resort to scouring the real estate market in search of sellers so desperate to sell that they or their lenders don't require any down payment. We assume neither.

So how do you get started in real estate if you don't want to own distressed properties in the worst neighborhoods, and you don't have a six-figure balance in your bank account to pay top dollar in the best neighborhoods? You embrace a long-term vision. You don't have to be wealthy or have great savings to make attractive real estate investments. In this book, we present a wide range of investment options, so there's something for virtually everyone's budget and personal situation. Our method of building real estate wealth over time is to create investment returns that are sustainable and provide generous returns on your investments.

Cash Requirements

In the following sections, we discuss the realities of the cash requirements to be a successful real estate investor.

Forget the myth of no money down

To invest in real estate, you need capital, and likewise you need a source from which to gather said capital. On late-night infomercials, at seminars, and in some books, you may hear self-appointed real estate experts tell you that you can invest in real estate with no money. And if that's not enticing enough, you may hear that you can buy properties where the seller will put cash in your hands.

Have such no-money-down situations ever existed among the billions of completed real estate transactions in the history of the modern world? Why, yes, they have. Realistically, can you find such opportunities among the best real estate investing options available to you? Why, no, you can't.

The perfect real estate investment doesn't exist. If you use our sensible criteria when seeking out properties that will be good real estate investments and then add the requirement that you can only make such investments with no money down, you'll waste years searching to no avail. We've never made a no-money-down real estate investment because the best properties simply aren't available on that basis.

The no-money-down properties we've seen aren't properties we want to own. And if you receive cash out of escrow upon closing on a property, you're either buying a severely distressed property that will soon require major cash infusions or you've overleveraged the property. If it sounds too good to be true, it *is* too good to be true!

What you need to get started

Most of the time, real estate investors make a down payment and borrow the majority of the money needed to complete a purchase. That's the conventional way to purchase real estate investment properties and will be the most successful method for you in the long run.

To qualify for the most attractive financing, lenders typically require that your down payment be at least 20 percent of the property's purchase price. The best investment property loans sometimes require 25 to 30 percent down for the most favorable terms. Lenders tend to be more conservative and require larger down payments during periods of falling real estate prices.

For most residential investment properties, such as single-family homes, attached housing such as condos and townhomes, and small apartment buildings of up to four units, you can get access to the best financing terms by making at least a 20 to 25 percent down payment. (Mortgages on non-owner-occupied property tend to be ¼ to ½ percent higher). You may be able to make smaller down payments (as low as 10 percent or less), but you'll pay much higher interest rates and loan fees, including private mortgage insurance (see Chapter 5).

You won't find such wonderful financing options for larger apartment buildings (five or more units), commercial real estate, and raw land. Compared with residential properties of up to four units, such investment property generally requires more money down and/or higher interest rates and loan fees. See Chapter 5 for more details.

Determining how much cash you need to close on a purchase is largely a function of the negotiated purchase price, including all closing costs and fees. Suppose you're looking to buy some modest residential housing for $100,000. For a 25 percent down payment, you need $25,000, and adding in another 5 percent for closing costs brings you to $30,000. If you have your heart set on buying a property that costs three times as much ($300,000), you need to triple these amounts to a total of about $90,000 for the best financing options.

Save the Required Cash

Most successful real estate investors get started building their real estate investment portfolio the old-fashioned way — through saving money and then gradually buying properties over the years. Many people have difficulty saving money because they don't know how to or are simply unwilling to limit their spending. Easy access to consumer debt (through credit cards and auto loans) creates huge obstacles to saving more and spending less.

Investing in real estate requires self-control, sacrifice, and discipline. Like most good things in life, you must be patient and plan ahead to be able to invest in real estate.

If you're not satisfied with how much of your monthly earnings you're able to save, you have two options:

- **Boost your income:** To increase your take-home pay, working more may be a possibility, or you may be able to take a more lucrative career path. Our main advice on this topic is to keep your priorities in order. You shouldn't put your personal health and relationships on the back burner for a workaholic schedule. We also believe in investing in your education. Education is key not only for your chosen profession but also for real estate investing. Consider getting a real estate license or learn to be an appraiser or property manager — skills that not only help you with your property investing but also may allow you to take on part-time work to supplement your income.

- **Reduce your spending:** For most people, this is the path to increased savings. Start by analyzing how much you expend on food, clothing, transportation, insurance, and other areas each month. After you have the data, decide where and how you want to cut back.

_____

_____

_____

Although the possibilities to reduce your spending are many, you and only you can decide which options you're willing and able to implement.

Overcome Down Payment Limitations

Most people, especially when they make their first real estate purchase, are strapped for cash. If you don't have 20-plus percent of the purchase price, don't panic — you can still own real estate. We have some solutions — you can either change your approach, allowing you more time to save or lowering your entry fees, or you can seek other sources of funding. In the following sections, we lay out your options.

Change your approach

Some ways you can alter your approach without having to find money elsewhere are as follows:

- **Seek low-money-down loans with private mortgage insurance:** Some lenders may offer you a mortgage even though you may be able to put down only 10 percent of the purchase price. These lenders will likely require you to purchase *private mortgage insurance* (PMI) for your loan. This insurance generally costs several hundred dollars per year and protects the lender if you default on your loan. (When you have at least 20 percent equity in the property, you can generally eliminate the PMI.)

- **Delay your gratification:** If you don't want the cost and strain of extra fees and bad mortgage terms, postpone your purchase. Boost your savings rate. Examine your current spending habits and plan to build up a nest egg to use to invest in your first rental. Often real estate investors get started by buying a new home and simply keeping their old home as a rental.

- **Think smaller:** Consider lower-priced properties. Smaller properties and ones that need some major work can help keep down the purchase price and the required down payment. For example, a duplex where you live in one unit and rent out the other is a cost-effective way to get started. We know many people who have used this entry strategy into rental property ownerships to achieve two goals: an owner-occupied place to live and a rental property that is convenient to manage.

- **Turn to low-entry-cost options:** For the ultimate in low-entry costs while adding real estate to your investment allocation strategy, *real estate investment trusts* (REITs) are best. These stock exchange-traded securities (which can also be bought through REIT-focused mutual funds and EFTs [exchange-traded funds]) can be bought into for several thousand dollars or less (you can invest even less in ETFs). REIT mutual funds can often be purchased for $1,000 or less inside retirement accounts.

  Lease options represent another low-cost (although more complicated) opportunity. With these, you begin by renting a property you may be interested in purchasing down the road. In the interim, a portion of your monthly rental payment goes toward the future purchase price. If you can find a seller willing to provide financing, you can keep your down payment to a minimum.

Tap into other common cash sources

Saving money from your monthly earnings will probably be the foundation for your real estate investing program. However, you may have access to other financial resources for down payments.

Dip into your retirement savings

Some employers allow you to borrow against your retirement account balance, under the condition that you repay the loan within a set number of years. Subject to eligibility requirements, first-time homebuyers can make penalty-free withdrawals of up to $10,000 from IRA accounts. (*Note:* You still must pay regular income tax on the withdrawal, which can significantly reduce the cash available.)

Borrow against home equity

Most real estate investors begin building their real estate portfolio after they buy their own home. Conservatively tapping into your home's equity may be a good down payment source for your property investments.

You can generally obtain a mortgage at a lower interest rate on your home than you can on investment property.

The smaller the risk to the lender, the lower its required return, and thus, the better rate for you as the borrower. Lenders view rental property as a higher risk proposition and for good reason: They know that when finances go downhill and the going gets tough, people pay their home mortgage to avoid losing the roof over their heads before they pay debts on a rental property.

Unless your current mortgage was locked in at lower rates than are available today, we generally recommend refinancing the first trust deed loan and freeing up equity that way versus taking out a home equity loan or line of credit.

A variation on the borrowing-against-home-equity idea uses the keep-your-original-home-as-a-rental strategy. You build up significant equity in your owner-occupied home and then decide to purchase a new home. Refinance the existing home (while you still live there for the best owner-occupied rates) and then convert it into a rental. Take the tax-free proceeds from the refinance and use that as the down payment on your new owner-occupied home.

Before you go running out to borrow to the maximum against your home, be sure that you

- **Can handle the larger payments:** Don't borrow more than the value of your home to invest in more real estate. The excessive leverage is dangerous and could come back to haunt you.

- **Understand the tax ramifications of all your alternatives:** Borrowing more against your home at what appears to be a slightly lower rate may end up costing you more after taxes if some of the borrowing isn't tax deductible. Under current tax laws, interest paid on home mortgages (first and second homes) of up to $1 million is tax deductible. You may also deduct the interest on home equity loans of up to $100,000.

  Be careful to understand the tax-deductibility issue when you refinance a home mortgage and borrow more than you originally had outstanding on the prior loan. If any of the extra amount borrowed isn't used to buy, build, or improve your primary or secondary residence, the deductibility of the interest on the excess amount borrowed is limited. Specifically, you may not deduct the interest on the extra amount borrowed that exceeds the $100,000 home equity limit.

- **Fully comprehend the risks of losing your home to foreclosure:** The more you borrow against your home, the greater the risk that you may lose the roof over your head to foreclosure should you not be able to make your mortgage payments. Although you need to use your cash for investing in and improving real estate, always keep some cash in a checking or money market rainy day account (for example for a new roof, painting, and so on) and not cutting things so close that you could lose it all.

Move financial investments into property investments

As you gain more comfort and confidence as a real estate investor, you may want to redirect some of your dollars from other investments like stocks, bonds, mutual funds, and ETFs into property. If you do, be mindful of the following:

- **Diversification:** Real estate is one of the prime investments (the others being stocks and small business) for long-term appreciation potential. Be sure you understand your portfolio's overall asset allocation and risk when making changes. See Chapter 1 for more details.

- **Tax issues:** If you've held other investments for more than one year, you can take advantage of the low long-term capital gains tax rates if you now want to sell. The maximum federal tax rate for so-called *long-term capital gains* (investments sold for more than they were purchased for after more than 12 months) is now 20 percent. Investors in the two lowest federal income tax brackets of 10 percent and 15 percent enjoy a 0 percent long-term capital gains tax rate. Try to avoid selling appreciated investments within the first year of ownership. Be sure to check on the latest tax laws because there's no guarantee these rates will continue in the future.

5

Financing Your Purchase

We know property investors who spent dozens to hundreds of hours finding the best locations and properties only to have their deals unravel when they were unable to gain approval for needed financing. You can't play if you can't pay.

This chapter covers the financing options you should consider. We explain how to select the mortgage that is most appropriate for the property you're buying and your overall personal and financial situation. In Chapter 6, we cover the process of applying for and locking up the specific loan you want.

Mortgage Options

Although you can find thousands of different types of mortgages, only two major categories of mortgages exist: fixed interest rate and adjustable rate. This section discusses these major loan types, what features they typically have, and how you can compare them with each other and select the one that best fits with your investment property purchases.

Fixed-rate mortgages

Fixed-rate mortgages, which are typically for a 15- or 30-year term for single-family properties, condos, and one- to four-unit apartments, have interest rates that remain constant over the life of the loan. Because the interest rate stays the same, your monthly mortgage payment stays the same.

The pros and cons

For purposes of making future estimates of your property's cash flow, fixed-rate mortgages offer you certainty and some peace of mind because you know precisely the size of your mortgage payment next month, next year, and ten years from now. But this piece of mind comes at a price:

- You generally pay a premium, in the form of a higher interest rate, compared with loans that have an adjustable interest rate over time. If you're buying a property and planning to improve it and sell it within five to ten years, you may be throwing money away by taking out a fixed-rate loan to lock in an interest rate for decades.

- If, like most investment property buyers, you're facing a tough time generating a healthy positive cash flow in the early years of owning a particular investment property, a fixed-rate mortgage is going to make it even more financially challenging. An adjustable-rate mortgage, by contrast, can lower your property's carrying costs in those early years. (We discuss adjustable-rate mortgages in the next section.)

- Fixed-rate loans carry the risk that if interest rates fall significantly after you obtain your mortgage and you're unable to refinance, you're stuck with a relatively higher-cost mortgage. For example, you may be unable to refinance if you lose your job, your employment income declines, the value of your property decreases, or the property's rental income slides. Even if you're able to refinance, you'll probably have to spend significant time and money to do so.

Comparing fixed rates

In addition to the ongoing, constant interest rate charged on a fixed-rate mortgage, lenders also typically levy an upfront fee, called points, which can be considered prepaid interest. *Points* are generally a percentage of the amount borrowed. To illustrate, 1.5 points are equal to 1.5 percent of the loan amount. So, for example, on a $200,000 mortgage, 1.5 points translate into $3,000 upfront (also known as prepaid) interest. Points can add significantly to the cost of borrowing money, particularly if you don't plan to keep the loan for long.

Generally speaking, the more points you pay on a given loan, the lower the ongoing interest rate the lender charges on that loan. That's why you can't compare various lenders' fixed-rate loans to one another unless you know the exact points on each specific mortgage, in addition to that loan's ongoing interest rate.

The following are two approaches to dealing with points, given your financial situation and investment goals:

- **Minimize the points:** When you're running low on cash to close on a mortgage, or if you don't plan to hold the loan or property for long, you probably want to keep your points (and other loan fees) to a minimum. You may want to take a higher interest rate on your mortgage.

- **Pay more points:** If you're more concerned with keeping your ongoing costs low, plan to hold the property for many years, and aren't cash constrained to close on the loan now, consider paying more points to lower your interest rate. This is known as *buying down the loan rate* and can be an excellent strategy to lower your overall costs of borrowing and increase the property's cash flow and equity buildup.

To make an easier apples-to-apples comparison of mortgages from different lenders, get interest rate quotes at the same point level. For example, ask each lender for the interest rate on a particular fixed-rate mortgage for which you pay 1 point or 2 points, for example. You may also compare the *annual percentage rate* (APR), which is a summary loan cost measure that includes all of a loan's fees and costs. However, remember that the APR assumes that you hold the mortgage for its entire term — such as 15 or 30 years. If you end up keeping the loan for a shorter time period, either because you refinance or pay off the mortgage early, the APR isn't valid and accurate (unless you recalculate based on the changed term and payoff).

Adjustable-rate mortgages (ARMs)

Adjustable-rate mortgages (ARMs) carry an interest rate that varies over time. An ARM starts with a particular interest rate, usually a good deal lower than the going rate on comparable length (15- or 30-year) fixed-rate mortgages, and then you pay different rates for every year during a 30-year mortgage. Because the interest rate on an ARM changes over time, so does the size of the loan's monthly payment.

ARMs are often attractive for a number of reasons:

- You can start paying your mortgage with a relatively low initial interest rate compared with fixed-rate loans. Given the economics of a typical investment property purchase, ARMs better enable an investor to achieve a positive cash flow in the early years of property ownership.

- Should interest rates decline, you can realize most, if not all, of the benefits of lower rates without the cost and hassle of refinancing. With a fixed-rate mortgage, the only way to benefit from an overall decline in the market level of interest rates is to refinance.

ARMs come with many more features and options than do fixed-rate mortgages, including caps, indexes, margins, and adjustment periods. The following sections help you to understand these important ARM features.

Start rate

The *start rate* on an ARM is the interest rate the mortgage begins with. Don't be fooled though: You don't pay this often tantalizingly low rate for too long. That is why it's often called a *teaser rate*. The start rate on most ARMs is set artificially low to entice you. In other words, even if the market level of interest rates doesn't change, your ARM is destined to increase as soon as the terms of the loan allow. An increase of 1 or 2 percentage points is common. The formula for determining the future interest rates on an ARM and rate caps is far more important in determining what a mortgage is going to cost you in the long run.

Future interest rate

ARMs are based on the following formula:

Future Interest Rate = Index + Margin

The *index* is a designated measure of the market interest rate that the lender chooses to calculate the specific interest rate for your loan. Indexes are generally quoted in the financial press. The *margin* is the amount added to the index to determine the interest rate you pay on your mortgage.

For example, suppose the loan you're considering uses a one-year Treasury bill index, which say is at about 2 percent, and the loan you're considering has a margin of 2.75 percent (also often referred to as 275 *basis points;* 100 basis points equals 1 percent). Thus, the following formula would drive the rate of this mortgage:

One - Year Treasury Bill Rate (2 percent) + Margin (2.75 percent)

Do the math and you get 4.75 percent. This figure is known as the *fully indexed rate* (the rate the loan has after the initial rate expires and if the index stays constant). If this loan starts out at 2 percent, you know that if the one-year Treasury bill index remains at the same level, your loan can increase to 4.75 percent. If this index rises 1 to 3 percent during the period that you're covered by the ARM's start rate, that means the loan's fully indexed rate goes to 5.75 percent $(3.00 + 2.75)$, which is nearly 3 percent higher than the loan's start rate.

Compare the fully indexed rate on an ARM you're considering to the current rate for a comparable term fixed-rate loan. You may see that the fixed-rate loan is at about the same interest rate, which may lead you to reconsider your choice of an ARM that carries the risk of rising to a higher future level.

Future interest rate adjustments

After the initial interest rate ends, the interest rate on an ARM fluctuates based on the loan formula. Typically, ARM interest rates change every 6 or 12 months, but some adjust every month. In advance of each adjustment, the lender sends you a notice telling you your new rate. Be sure to check these notices because on rare occasions, lenders make mistakes.

Almost all ARMs come with a rate cap, which limits the maximum rate change (up or down) allowed at each adjustment. This limit is usually referred to as the *adjustment cap*. On most loans that adjust every six months, the adjustment cap is 1 percent; the interest rate charged on the mortgage can move up or down no more than 1 percentage point in an adjustment period.

Loans that adjust more than once per year usually limit the maximum rate change that's allowed over the entire year as well — known as the *annual rate cap*. On the vast majority of such loans, 2 percent is the annual rate cap. Likewise, almost all ARMs come with *lifetime caps,* which represent the highest rate allowed over the entire life of the loan. Lifetime caps of 5 to 6 percent higher than the initial start rate are common for adjustables.

Taking an ARM without rate caps is like heading out for a weeklong outdoor trek without appropriate rain gear and clothing for varying temperatures. When you consider an adjustable-rate mortgage, you must identify the maximum payment that you can handle. If you can't handle the payment that comes with a 10 or 11 percent interest rate, for example, don't look at ARMs that may go that high. As you crunch the numbers to see what your property's cash flow looks like under different circumstances, consider calculating how your mortgage payment changes based on various higher interest rates.

Common Fees

Whether the loan is fixed or adjustable, mortgage lenders typically assess other upfront fees and charges. The lender must disclose these ancillary fees. You may have to search to find them in the paperwork, so make sure you do because they can add up to quite a bundle with some lenders. Here's our take on the typical extra charges you're likely to encounter and what's reasonable and what's not:

- **Application fee:** Most lenders charge several hundred dollars to work with you to complete your paperwork and see it through their loan evaluation process. Should your loan be rejected, or if it's approved and you decide not to take it, the lender needs to cover its costs. Some lenders credit or return this fee to you upon closing their loan, but you need to verify it upfront in writing.

- **Credit report charge:** Most lenders charge you for the cost of obtaining your credit report, which tells the lender whether you've filed bankruptcy in the last seven years, plus repaid other loans, including *consumer debt* (such as credit cards, auto loans, and so on), on time. A credit report also allows the lender to verify your employment and personal residence and business addresses. Your credit report should cost about $50 for each individual or entity that will be a borrower.

- **Appraisal fee:** The property for which you borrow money needs to be valued. If you default on your mortgage, a lender doesn't want to get stuck with a property that's worth less than you owe. The cost for a standard form appraisal typically ranges from several hundred dollars for most residential properties of one to four units to as much as $1,000 or more for larger investment properties. You may be able to save some money if the property has been appraised recently and you contact the appraiser and he's willing and able to provide you with an updated appraisal.

- **Environmental assessment or phase I:** Virtually all lenders making loans on residential properties with five or more units or, especially, commercial property, require a qualified engineering company to perform a site assessment and overview of the entire area in which the property is located to identify possible environmental issues. This type of report is commonly referred to as a *phase I environmental report,* and the cost correlates to the location, type of property, size, and even the prior use of the property and the surrounding area. Phase I reports can run from $300 to as much as tens of thousands of dollars.

- **Third-party physical inspection:** Depending on the property being financed, lenders often require third-party inspections by competent professionals. For example, an inspection report from a licensed pest control firm documenting the property condition and the presence of termites and/or wood-destroying organisms is required in virtually all transactions, including single-family homes and commercial properties. Again, the cost of these reports varies depending on the property.

Request a detailing of other fees and charges in writing from all lenders that you're seriously considering. You need to know the total of all lender fees so you can accurately compare different lenders' loans and determine how much closing on your loan will cost you. For residential and commercial income properties, the lender usually asks for a deposit that the lender uses to cover the types of fees and charges outlined here.

To reduce the possibility of wasting your time and money applying for a mortgage that you may not qualify for, ask the lender for any reasons it may not approve you. Disclose any problems on your credit report or with the property. Don't expect the lender to provide you with a list of credit or property problems that may conceivably put the kibosh on a mortgage.

Making Some Mortgage Decisions

You can't spend months deciding which mortgage may be right for your situation. So in this section, we help you zero in on which type is best for you.

Choosing between fixed and adjustable

Choosing between a fixed-rate or adjustable-rate loan is an important decision in the real estate investment process. Consider the advantages and disadvantages of each mortgage type and decide what's best for your situation before going out to refinance or purchase real estate. This section covers the key factors to consider.

Your ability and desire to accept financial risk

How much risk can you handle in regard to the size of your property's monthly mortgage payment? If you can take the financial risks that come with an ARM, you have a better chance of saving money and maximizing your property's cash flow with an adjustable-rate rather than a fixed-rate loan. Your interest rate starts lower and stays lower with an ARM, if the overall level of interest rates stays unchanged. Even if rates go up, they'll likely come back down over the life of your loan. If you can stick with your ARM for better and for worse, you should come out ahead in the long run.

ARMs make more sense if you borrow less than you're qualified for. If your income (and applicable investment property cash flow) significantly exceeds your spending, you may feel less anxiety about the fluctuating interest rate on an ARM. If you do choose an adjustable loan, you may feel more financially secure if you have a hefty financial cushion (at least six months' to as much as a year's worth of expenses reserved) that you can access if rates go up.

If you can't afford the highest-allowed payment on an ARM, don't take one. You shouldn't take the chance that the rate may not rise that high — it can, and you can lose the property.

Ask your lender to calculate the highest possible monthly payment that your loan allows. The number the lender comes up with is the payment that you face if the interest rate on your loan goes to the highest level allowed, or the *lifetime cap.* (For more on caps, see the "Future interest rate adjustments" section earlier in the chapter.)

Don't take an adjustable mortgage because the lower initial interest rate allows you to afford the property that you want to buy (unless you're certain that your income and property cash flow will enable you to meet future payment increases). Try setting your sights on a property that you can afford to buy with a fixed-rate mortgage.

Length of time you expect to keep the mortgage

Saving interest on most ARMs is usually a certainty in the first two or three years. An adjustable-rate mortgage starts at a lower interest rate than a fixed one. But, if rates rise, you can end up repaying the savings that you achieve in the early years of the mortgage.

If you aren't going to keep your mortgage for more than five to seven years, you pay more interest to carry a fixed-rate mortgage. A mortgage lender takes extra risk in committing to a fixed-interest rate for 15 to 30 years. Lenders don't know what may happen in the intervening years, so they charge you a premium in case interest rates move significantly higher in future years.

Selecting short-term or long-term

Most mortgage lenders offer you the option of 15-year or 30-year mortgages. So how do you decide whether a shorter- or longer-term mortgage is best for your investment property purchase?

To afford the monthly payments and have a positive cash flow, many investment property buyers need to spread their mortgage loan payments over a longer period of time, and a 30-year mortgage is the way to do it. A 15-year mortgage has higher monthly payments because you pay it off quicker. At a fixed-rate mortgage interest rate of 7 percent, for example, a 15-year mortgage comes with payments that are about 35 percent higher than those for a 30-year mortgage.

Don't consider a 15-year mortgage unless you're sure you can afford the higher payments. Even if you can afford these higher payments, taking the 15-year option isn't necessarily better.

You may be able to find better uses for the money. If you can earn a higher rate of return investing your extra cash versus paying the interest on your mortgage, for instance, you may come out ahead investing your money rather than paying down your mortgage faster.

 If you decide on a 30-year mortgage, you still maintain the flexibility to pay the mortgage off faster. You can choose to make larger-than-necessary payments and create your own 15-year mortgage. However, you can fall back to making only the payments required on your 30-year schedule when the need arises.

Typically the interest rate will be lower for a 15-year loan than a 30-year loan, but if they're the same or very close, then you gain the flexibility with a 30-year loan. You can then adjust your payments over the life of the loan to customize your loan to exactly the term you desire.

6

Mortgages

In Chapter 5, we discuss how to choose among the many loan options available to select the one that best suits your personal and financial situation. In the process of delving into the different types of real estate investment financing, you may have already begun the process of speaking with different lenders and surfing websites.

In this chapter, we provide our top tips and advice for shopping for and securing the best financing you can for your real estate investment purchases and refinances. We also cover common loan problems that may derail your plans.

Shopping for Mortgages

Financing costs of your real estate investment purchases are generally the single biggest expense by far, so it pays to shop around and know how to unearth the best deals. You may find that many lenders would love to have your business, especially if you have a strong credit rating. Although having numerous lenders competing for your business can save you money, it can also make mortgage shopping and selection difficult. This section should help you simplify matters.

Referrals

Many sources of real estate advice simply tell you to get referrals in your quest to find the best mortgage lenders. Sounds simple and straightforward — but it's not. For instance, loans for commercial investment properties and residential rental properties with five or more units have different lender underwriting requirements and terms compared with residential one- to four-unit loans.

 Good referrals can be a useful tool for locating the best lenders. Here are a few sources we recommend:

- Start with a bank or credit union that you have a relationship with and then seek referrals from it if it's not interested in making the specific loan you have in mind.

_____

_____

_____

- Collect referrals from people who you know and trust and who have demonstrated some ability to select good service providers. Start with professional service providers (tax advisors, lawyers, financial planners, real estate agents, and so on) you know and respect, and ask them for their recommendations.

- Contact associations of real estate investors, especially those in your state. (You can find a comprehensive list organized by state at the website www.realestateassociations.com.)

Don't take anyone's referrals as gospel. Always be wary of business people who refer you to folks who have referred business to them over the years. You want to make sure the referral is not just a payback or reciprocal arrangement with no justification, but someone who warrants consideration.

Mortgage brokers

You don't need to use a mortgage broker unless you're trying to get a loan for a property that has some challenges or you as the buyer have less than stellar credit or want to put the minimum down. Mortgage brokers also may not be justified when the market conditions are favorable and many lenders are seeking to make loans. In these instances, we recommend going directly to lenders for simple deals and using mortgage brokers for bigger, more complicated, or more difficult deals and especially if the capital markets are tight and lenders aren't motivated to make deals.

Many property buyers get a headache trying to shop among the enormous universe of mortgages and lenders. Check out the following sections when deciding whether you want to use a broker.

A broker's contributions

A good mortgage broker can make the following contributions to your real estate investing team:

- **Advice:** If you're like most people, you may have a difficult time deciding which type of mortgage is best for your situation. A good mortgage broker can take the time to listen to your financial and personal situation and goals and offer suggestions for specific loans that match your situation.

- **Shopping:** Even after you figure out the specific type of mortgage that you want, dozens (if not hundreds) of lenders may offer that type of loan. (You'll find fewer lender options for five-plus-unit residential properties and commercial properties.)

Thoroughly shopping among the options to find the best mortgage takes time and knowledge you may lack. A good mortgage broker can save you time and money by shopping for your best deal. Brokers can be especially helpful if you have a less than pristine credit report or you want to buy property with a low down payment.

- **Paperwork:** An organized and detail-oriented mortgage broker can assist you with completing the morass of forms most lenders demand. The paperwork can be overwhelming and tedious if you haven't been through the process before and your records aren't in order. Mortgage brokers and escrow officers can assist you with preparing your loan package so you put your best foot forward with lenders.

Have your personal financial statement prepared in advance so it can be easily updated. Each time you seek a loan for an investment property, you have to provide a current financial statement to the broker.

_____

_____

_____

- **Closing the deal:** After you sign a purchase agreement to buy a real estate investment property, you still have a lot to do before you're the proud new property owner (see Chapter 10). A competent mortgage broker makes sure you meet the important deadlines for closing the deal.

Commissions and other contingencies

A mortgage broker typically gets paid a percentage, usually between 0.5 and 1 percent, of the loan amount. This commission is negotiable, especially on larger loans that are more lucrative. Don't confuse the mortgage broker commission with the lender-required points. When lenders have a lot of money to place, you may find that using a mortgage broker doesn't cost you the full amount of their quoted commission because lenders will reduce their points by enough to cover a portion or even all of the mortgage broker fees.

The mortgage broker may also be receiving compensation from certain lenders, which further complicates your analysis. It also means you need to explore the fee structure with each proposed loan. Be sure to ask what the commission is on every alternative loan that a broker pitches.

Even if you plan to shop on your own, talking to a mortgage broker may be worthwhile. At the very least, you can compare what you find with what brokers say they can get for you. Again, be careful. Some brokers tell you what you want to hear — that is, that they can beat your best find — and then aren't able to deliver when the time comes.

If your loan broker quotes you a really good deal, ask who the lender is. Most brokers refuse to reveal this information until you pay the necessary fee to cover the appraisal, credit report, and required environmental reports. But after taking care of those fees, you can check with the lender to verify the interest rate, the points, and the amortization term that the broker quotes you, and make sure you're eligible for the loan.

Finding mortgages online

You can shop for just about anything and everything online, so why should mortgages be any different? Mortgage websites often claim that they save you lots of time and money.

In our experience, the Internet is better used for mortgage research than for securing a specific mortgage. That's not to say that some sites can't provide competitive loans in a timely fashion. However, we've seen property purchases fall apart because the buyers relied upon a website that failed to deliver a loan in time.

Here's a short list of some of our favorite mortgage-related websites that you may find helpful:

- **HSH Associates:** The folks at HSH Associates (www. hsh.com) collect mortgage information for most metropolitan areas.

- **Government-related sites:** The websites of the US Department of Housing and Urban Development (www.hud.gov) and the Veterans Administration (www.va.gov) provide information on government loan programs and feature foreclosed homes for sale.

  Fannie Mae, which stands for the Federal National Mortgage Association (www.fanniemae.com), and Freddie Mac, which is the Federal Home Loan Mortgage Corporation (www.freddiemac.com), have worked over the years with the federal government to support the mortgage marketplace.

- **Mortgage Bankers Association:** The trade association for mortgage lenders, the Mortgage Bankers Association (www.mbaa.org), has articles and data on the mortgage marketplace.

This group is an excellent source of information on loans for residential properties with five or more units and commercial, industrial, and retail properties.

- **E-LOAN:** One of the first major online lenders, E-LOAN has stood the test of time and continues to offer competitive loans (www.eloan.com). This well-organized site can give you a quick overview of competitive mortgage pricing. Of course, you're under no obligation to use one of its mortgages just because you survey the options available.

Common Borrowing Problems

The best defense against loan rejection is avoiding it in the first place. To head off potential rejection, disclose anything that may cause a problem *before* you apply for the loan.

Even if you're the ideal mortgage borrower in the eyes of every lender, you may encounter financing problems with some properties. And of course, not all real estate buyers have a perfect credit history, lots of spare cash, and no debt. If you're one of those borrowers who must jump through more hoops than others to get a loan, don't give up hope. Few borrowers are perfect from a lender's perspective, and many problems aren't that difficult to fix.

Poor credit history

Late payments, missed payments, or debts that you never bothered to pay can tarnish your credit report and squelch a lender's desire to offer you a mortgage loan. If you've been turned down for a loan because of your less-than-stellar credit history, request a free copy of your credit report from the lender that turned you down.

Getting a report before you even apply for a loan is advisable. Once a year, you're entitled to obtain a free copy of your credit report from each of the three credit bureaus. The contact information for the credit bureaus is

- **Equifax:** 800-685-1111; www.equifax.com
- **Experian:** 888-397-3742; www.experian.com
- **Transunion:** 800-916-8800; www.transunion.com

If problems are accurately documented on your credit report, try to explain them to your lender. Getting the bum's rush? Call other lenders and tell them your credit problems upfront and see whether you can find one willing to offer you a loan. Mortgage brokers may also be able to help you shop for lenders in these cases.

As for erroneous information listed on your credit report, call the credit bureaus. If specific creditors are the culprits, call them too. They're required to submit any new information or correct any errors at once. Keep notes from your conversations and make sure you put your case in writing and add your comments to your credit report.

Another common credit problem is having too much *consumer debt* at the time you apply for a mortgage. The more credit card, auto loan, and other consumer debt you rack up, the less mortgage you qualify for. If you're turned down for the mortgage, consider it a wake-up call to get rid of this high-cost debt.

Insufficient income

If you're self-employed or have changed jobs, your income may not resemble your past income, or your income may not be what a mortgage lender needs to see relative to the amount that you want to borrow. A simple (although not always feasible) way around this is to make a larger down payment.

If you can't make a large down payment, another option is to get a cosigner for the loan. As long as the person you choose isn't overextended himself, he may be able to help you qualify for a larger loan than you can get on your own. Make sure you put your agreement in writing so no misunderstandings occur.

7

Location, Location, Value

Merely owning real estate isn't the key to success in real estate investing; acquiring and owning the right real estate at the right price is the way to build wealth! As you gain experience in real estate, you'll develop your own strategy, but to make any strategy succeed, you need to do your homework and evaluate both the positive and negative aspects of your proposed real estate investment. That's where we come in.

In this chapter, we help you know where to buy property, explain how to find properties that you can easily add value to, and discuss real estate cycles and timing.

Deciding Where to Invest

If you're going to invest in real estate, you need to decide on a location. Most real estate investors initially — and wisely — look in their local communities.

 Stay close to home with your real estate investments — no more than one to two hours away by your favorite mode of transportation.

Although virtually everyone lives in an area with opportunities for real estate investing, not everyone lives in an area where the prospects are good for real estate in general. That's why it's important to broaden your geographic investment horizon as long as you don't compromise your ability to effectively manage and control your property.

If you decide to invest in real estate in your own locale, you still need to do tons of research to decide where and what to buy. Keep in mind, though, that you can spend the rest of your life looking for the *perfect* real estate investment, never find it, never invest, and miss out on lots of opportunities, profit, and even fun.

_____

_____

_____

Value-Added Properties

With investment real estate, you're looking for properties that allow you to make physical and/or fiscal improvements that will ultimately lower the expected cap rate to a future investor, which is essentially lowering the required rate of return because you have removed much of the risk. You want to buy when you determine that the property has a strong likelihood of producing future increases in net operating income (NOI) and cash flow. So you should look for properties where the income can be increased or the expenses reduced.

As you look for a rental property, many sellers and their real estate brokers will assure you that the current rents are really too low and that there is tremendous upside in the property to be tapped simply by buying the property and raising the rents. If it were that easy, why wouldn't the current owner raise the rent and then sell the property for a higher price?

If you research the market, you'll identify certain clues that indicate whether a property really has rents that are below market. Properties with no vacancies and a waiting list are prime candidates. Other telltale signs are properties that have low turnover and then have multiple applicants for those rare vacancies. Economics 101 says that if demand exceeds supply, the price is too low.

Some owners market their real estate investment properties at a below-market price. These are motivated sellers, probably with a variety of personal reasons for their need to sell more quickly and cheaply than they would if they had more time and patience.

Some sellers don't achieve the top value in the market for other reasons. For example, some owners despise the process of selling their rental properties so much that they knowingly underprice the property to ensure a quick and clean transaction and retain the ability to reject any contingencies that a buyer would typically require in a *market deal*. The elimination of hassling and haggling is paramount to these sellers; they just want to complete the sale, so they're willing to give the buyer such a good deal that the buyer takes the property essentially as-is.

Real estate investors often ask, "How do I find these underpriced properties?" Our experience indicates that underpriced investment properties typically have older owners with no mortgage who have exhausted the possibility of taking depreciation deductions on their tax returns.

Look for properties where you can increase value. These *value-added properties* allow you to either increase the NOI or decrease the rate and thus create value. The value of a property is increased with an increase in NOI or a decrease in the capitalization rate. The capitalization rate is directly correlated to the anticipated risk of the investment, so stabilizing properties through long-term leases and more financially viable tenants can reduce risk and lead to a lower cap rate and a higher value.

A simple example of how to increase the value of a building is to find a residential rental property in a high-demand area where all rental rates are the same for similar floor plans. In reality, the rents should reflect the fact that, say, not all two-bedroom units have the same location benefits. For example, a unit overlooking the pool is often more desirable than a unit on the main street, so raising the rents for the more desirable units increases rental income.

Seller's and Buyer's Markets

Some real estate investors make the mistake of not continuing to research the economics of their real estate markets after they've made their investments. Even if you plan to buy and hold, you need to pay attention to the market conditions.

Savvy real estate investors monitor the markets and look for the telltale signs of real estate cycles. These cycles present opportunities for expanding your real estate portfolio or repositioning from weakening markets to strengthening markets because not all areas experience peaks and troughs at the same time. That is why you need to know and track the timing of seller's and buyer's markets.

Real estate cycles

Real estate markets are cyclical, and successful real estate investors remain aware of the real estate cycles in their areas. Two types of markets make up the real estate cycle:

- A **buyer's market** occurs when current property owners are unable to sell their properties quickly and must be more flexible on the price and terms.

- A **seller's market** is almost like the classic definition of inflation — "too much money chasing too few goods." In this case, the goods are real estate properties, which are in high demand. When sellers are receiving multiple offers within 24 to 48 hours of a listing or you see properties selling for more than the asking price, you're in a strong seller's market.

Real estate traditionally experiences cycles as the demand for real estate leads to a shortage of supply and higher rents and appreciation. That leads to the building of additional properties, which, along with changes in demand due to economic cycles, usually results in overbuilding and a decline in rents and property valuation.

Can real estate investors who track real estate cycles make investment decisions based on this information? Absolutely. Most successful and knowledgeable real estate investors see potential for increasing their real estate investment returns by timing the real estate market.

_____

_____

_____

Timing the real estate market

Although the length and depth of the real estate cycles vary, there are clear highs and lows that real estate investors need to consider.

A key factor to knowing when the market has hit a low is the *investment horizon,* or planned holding period for a particular investor and that specific investment. If the holding period is long enough, even purchasing income properties in a seemingly overpriced market will probably look good 15 to 20 years later.

The alternatives are to identify those markets with excellent economic fundamentals where prices have remained low and invest there. The concept is similar to the "buy low, sell high" truism for stocks, except you sell in overpriced markets and reinvest in the lower priced markets. Such markets do exist, but the question is whether the properties in the lower-priced markets are going to provide the same or better investment returns in the long run versus alternative markets.

Unlike the stock market, real estate transactions entail significant transaction costs (as a percentage of the market value of the property). That's why selling and buying property too frequently undermines your returns.

_____

_____

_____

It's our contention that even in the few markets where such "bargains" exist, they aren't really great opportunities. We are reminded of the business concept that in the long run you usually get what you pay for! There is so much more than just the projected rent and the selling price. Without going into a detailed analysis of property condition, expenses, and other invaluable criteria, you should consider whether these areas pass muster by performing an economic analysis.

Knowing when to sell and when to buy real estate is easier said than done. But if you follow the fundamentals of economic analysis, and remember that "location, location, value" is the key to successful real estate investing, you can do well.

8

Valuing Property

With the help of your real estate team, you should narrow your real estate investment opportunities down to those properties that seem to have the best chance to produce financially in the long run.

In this chapter, we explain how to run the numbers. We cover the essential elements of understanding and arriving at a property's income and expenses and net operating income (NOI) — and we explain what that is! We then show you the valuation tools used by appraisers and lenders to determine what a property is worth.

But after you've done all of your research and analysis, you still need to establish whether a proposed property has the potential to be a good investment opportunity. Overpaying for a good property isn't any better than getting a deal on a bad property. Neither will meet your goals. So we close the chapter by putting it all together to help you decide how much you should consider paying for a particular property.

Return on Investment

The purchase of an investment property is really the purchase of a future income stream or cash flow. Although the satisfaction of being the owner of a rental property may be an important issue for some people, most real estate investors focus on the investment returns that they can generate from a property.

Four elements determine the return you see on your investment:

- **Net cash flow:** *Net cash flow* is money generated by the property after deducting all costs and debt service from the income. See the "Cash Flow" section later in this chapter.

- **Tax benefits of depreciation:** Many investors are able to use these tax benefits to shelter other sources of income, which gives you in essence an interest-free loan by deferring taxes.

- **Buildup of equity:** If you acquired the property with debt, the equity buildup from paying down the debt over time is a factor.

- **Appreciation:** True wealth is created through *appreciation* (buying property and selling it years later for much more than you paid).

The key to generating a profitable real estate portfolio is finding and purchasing properties that exhibit the potential for high occupancy and growth in income while keeping expenses and turnover reasonable. Success in real estate investing depends on purchasing a property for the right price so you can use your management skills to increase the value over time.

You also need to determine what work needs to be done to the property to correct any deferred maintenance or curable functional obsolescence. Even if you simply hold the property and look for cash flow and appreciation, you want to be able to evaluate the holding costs during your ownership period.

Then you need to determine the future value of the property to calculate the likely disposition price and determine your return on investment.

Net Operating Income

Knowledgeable real estate investors begin a serious analysis of a potential property acquisition by determining the projected *net operating income,* commonly abbreviated as NOI.

The calculation of net operating income is simply

NOI = Gross Operating Income – Operating Expenses

NOI is the most critical factor in determining the potential for return on your investment in real estate. Determining a property's NOI is one of the fundamental building blocks to analyzing real estate investments. Any decision — to buy, hold, or sell — should only be made after a careful analysis of the *actual current* and *projected future* NOI for a given real estate investment. Arriving at a reasonable estimate for future NOI is the key to determining the value parameters for your real estate investment. We recommend that you value a property based on the projected NOI for the next year, or preferably next few years.

The current NOI is fairly easy to obtain and is often provided by the seller. Deriving the projected NOI is a more time-consuming and in-depth process. Many times, the estimation of NOI is based on several assumptions or projections about future events that are anything but certain. Will your tenants renew their leases (and at what rates)? Will the tenants make their rent payments and other contractual requirements as agreed in their leases? Will expenses stay within the expected range, or will there be significant world or local events that lead to a spike in costs?

Whether you receive current or projected NOI estimates from a seller, be careful to verify the numbers. Some sellers, and many real estate brokers and agents, prefer to provide a *pro forma NOI* (a *projection* of future financial performance of the property) that uses higher rents and lower expenses. These fictitious numbers are based on the hopeful theory that the new owner will raise the rents to market level and simultaneously lower the costs of operating the property. These assumptions are rarely valid.

Have you ever seen a projection from a seller, her broker, or her sales agent that projects a lower NOI for an investment property on the market? They act as if the only way for NOI to go is up. Although you want to invest in properties where that is the likely result, the reality is that real estate is a cyclical business, and supply-and-demand factors have a major impact.

Make a careful and detailed analysis of the property you're considering. Develop your own operating pro forma prior to purchasing any property. And any evaluation or projection of the income stream for a property should begin with an analysis of each lease or rental agreement.

Evaluating income

To evaluate the income side of your budget, we advise that you painstakingly record and verify all income by using a zero-based budget concept. A *zero-based budget* is where you start with a blank piece of paper (or spreadsheet) and individually, tenant by tenant, create the projected rents and income stream for the property.

Sellers may provide or be asked to sign a certified rent roll or comparable document verifying the accuracy of the tenants and rents listed. Use this document cautiously. Conduct your own independent analysis of the current and future rent payments due under the terms of the existing leases. Don't just gather static data and numbers on your current tenants; you must be able to interpret the data. Evaluate the strength of each tenant. The lease may give you the legal right to future rent payments; however, a tenant who is unable or unwilling to meet his lease obligations won't be good for your rental collections.

You want a property that has tenants who not only have the current financial strength to meet their obligations under the lease but who will also increase your income in future years.

Tenants are the key to your future success, and you want to make sure you can provide the proper environment so their businesses can grow and prosper while you benefit from their rental payments, which ultimately pay for the building you plan to own free-and-clear in the future.

The income side of the equation involves more than just estimating rents. The typical income and expense statements in real estate include standard terminology that all real estate investors should know:

- **Gross potential income** or GPI is the maximum gross income that would be generated from the rent if the property were at 100 percent occupancy and all money owed were collected in full.

- **Effective gross income** or EGI is essentially the money that is actually collected. EGI is calculated by taking the GPI and then subtracting the vacancies, concessions, delinquencies, and collection losses and then adding the other income from late charges, returned checks, and all other secondary or non-rent sources.

In the sections that follow, we provide the details on what to subtract and add to work your way from GPI to EGI.

Vacancies

The real estate investment community seems to be locked on using 5 percent as the vacancy factor; brokers and lenders typically use a 5 percent vacancy factor without any regard for the actual market conditions. This number may or may not be the right number to use; we advise that you carefully determine the most accurate estimate of future vacancy rather than use a standard figure such as 5 percent.

The issue of vacancies is particularly applicable to many new real estate investors who begin either by retaining their current homes as investment properties when they move up to larger homes or by purchasing rental properties as investments. Novice investors often simply compare the monthly rental rate that they plan on charging to the monthly costs for paying the mortgage and any other recurring expenses (property taxes, utilities, homeowner's dues, and so on). This practice can be dangerous if you don't have sufficient cash reserves for the unexpected — like being unable to find or retain tenants or having to evict a tenant who stops paying.

If you have a single-family rental home, the property is either occupied or vacant. With the average length of residential tenancies in many parts of the country at less than one year, using a 0 percent vacancy factor is unrealistic. Our suggestion for your pro forma for a single-family rental home is to anticipate a loss of income equivalent to one month per every twelve months, which reflects an 8.3 percent vacancy rate. This rate may represent a vacancy, a delinquency, or a concession (see the following sections), but one way or another, you're likely to lose at least one month's rent/income on average per year, and you should allow for this prospect in preparing your pro forma to determine the potential income before making your investment decision.

Concessions

A *concession* is any benefit or deal-sweetener offered by the landlord to entice the tenant to enter into a lease or rental agreement. Concessions can be anything of value that motivates the tenant, but most commonly include free or reduced rent or additional features. In many areas, concessions are a significant factor in estimating future income. A concession of one month's free rent is essentially an 8.3 percent discount of the annual rent. A free month's rent for a simple residential tenancy with a monthly rent of $1,000 means that you'll only collect $11,000 in the first year, or an effective rental rate of $916.66, or a concession rate of 8.3 percent. This reduction is a significant factor when added to your expected vacancy rate and allowance for collection loss.

Delinquencies and collection losses

The industry standard for *collection loss* (rent or other charges that the landlord must write off as uncollectible) is typically 0.5 percent of rental income. This is another number that seems to be acceptable as a general rule; however, savvy real estate investors make their own analyses of the actual collection loss they may experience based on the strength of the tenant, the strength and depth of the local job market, the average turnover of the area overall, the amount of security deposit they hold, and the nature of local tenant/landlord laws.

During a weak economic environment, collection loss can be even more significant, and prudent landlords take steps to make sure they have financially sound tenants who can pay rent. The competition for these qualified tenants means you may have to lower the rent or offer concessions, which are better options than trying to get top dollar from an unqualified tenant.

Additional income streams

In addition to rent, other types of payments are essential elements to your income stream. Other income items can consist of late charges, returned check charges, and various ancillary income items. The ancillary items depend on the type of investment property, but for residential properties, they can consist of laundry, parking, vending, storage, concierge service, and so on. Examples for commercial properties can include sources similar to those for residential properties, plus items like common area maintenance charges (CAM), supplemental HVAC (heating, ventilation, and air conditioning) charges, special security requirements, and telecommunications.

Tallying operating expenses

Just as you did with your income, use a zero-based budget concept to forecast the projected operating expenses for your property. Although historical expenses are worth reviewing, we recommend that you question every expense. You may find that the current landscaper is willing to charge you less just to keep the account. Or maybe you have contractors and vendors you already use who will charge you less.

The income and expense information presented by most owners or their real estate agents doesn't accurately reflect the current financial results. Inevitably, they may claim that the rents are too low, and they may show artificially lowered operating expenses in order to inflate NOI. As the potential purchaser of this property, you want to deal with reality, so be sure to require the seller to provide you with a copy of her federal tax return Schedule E for each year of her ownership — or at least the last several years. Rarely does the tax return overstate the income or understate the expenses of a rental property.

Utilities

Evaluate your utility costs as soon as you can because this expense is typically one of the larger costs of operating your property and is also subject to significant increases. Determine the current and projected rates for the utilities by contacting the service providers for electricity, natural gas, water and sewer, cable, waste removal, and any other utilities that are provided at the property. Virtually all of these utilities are regulated locally or at the state level and must file future rates in advance.

Thus, determining the future cost for utilities is relatively easy if your usage remains the same. But consider any energy and resource efficiency improvements that you can make, such as lighting, low-flow toilets, automated sprinklers, drip irrigation systems, and other ways to reduce the consumption and provide incentives for your tenants to conserve.

One sure way to get tenants to conserve is to make them responsible for paying for their own utility usage. This approach can dramatically improve your NOI, and it's often a win/win situation because many tenants make long-delayed energy-efficient changes to improve conservation practices.

Management fees

A common mistake made by many investors is failing to incorporate the value of their time if they self-manage their property. Your estimate of operating costs should include a management fee even if you self-manage. Your time is worth something, and there is an *opportunity cost* (whatever other productive activity you could be doing with that time) as well. Also, you may decide to hire a property manager so you can focus on the acquisition, improvement, and disposition of your real estate holdings. Including a comparable management fee now saves your projections from taking a hit later.

Insurance

Like utilities, property-casualty insurance is another major operating expense for which you need to get a specific quote for future projections instead of relying on historical data provided by the seller. Insurance coverage and rates can vary widely from one insurance company to another.

Other operating costs

Don't forget all of the other operating costs for your property, including your outside vendors that provide services. You may have landscaping, pest control, painting, janitorial, and other services. Contact each firm for pricing, and put these services out for competitive bids when you feel that the pricing and services offered aren't the best values.

Get current bids for all of the expenses of owning and maintaining your property. For maintenance, you can look at historic numbers, but you want to keep the building's age and condition in mind when setting your budget for upkeep.

Cash Flow

As you look at various properties that you may want to acquire, you discover that the real estate investment community always refers to the NOI of a given property and commonly uses that number to set the value or asking price of a property. The NOI tells you what you can afford to pay for the property. We show you the calculations in the "Net Operating Income" section earlier in this chapter.

However, don't confuse the NOI with *cash flow,* which is NOI minus debt service payments and capital expenditures (for example, new roof, appliances, floor coverings, and so on). In the example in Table 8-1, the Net Operating Income is $600,000, but the actual cash flow before taxes to the investor is $150,000.

After you have your NOI, you can project your annual cash flow. The formula is straightforward:

> NOI – Debt Service – Capital Improvements =
> Before-Tax Cash Flow

Annual gross potential rental income (GPI)	$1,000,000
Plus other income	20,000
Plus CAM reimbursement	30,000
Minus vacancy and collection loss	(50,000)
Effective gross income (EGI)	1,000,000
Operating expenses	(400,000)
Annual Net Operating Income (NOI)	**$600,000**
Annual debt service	(400,000)
Capital improvements	(50,000)
Annual Before-Tax Cash Flow	**$150,000**

Table 8-1: *Sample Investment Commercial Property Cash Flow*

Servicing debt

The *broker information sheet* (or sales flyer) on an available property may provide proposed financing. However, make sure that the *debt service* projection in your income and expense pro forma relies on a firm financing commitment that you have received.

Although the annual debt-service payments are a direct result of the amount of the purchase price borrowed, for most conventionally financed properties, the debt service will be 80 to 90 percent of the NOI in the early years of your ownership of the property. If you have fixed-rate financing, the debt service is going to be an easy number to plug into your income and expense pro forma because the payment won't change. However, if you have an adjustable-rate mortgage, you'll need to estimate future interest rates and debt service payments to calculate future cash flows.

Capital improvements

In developing their estimates or pro formas of projected financial results for a proposed investment property, many investors neglect to account for, or seriously underestimate the need for, capital improvements to the property. *Capital improvements* are the replacement of major building components or systems such as the roof, driveways, HVAC, windows, appliances, elevators, and floor and window coverings. Real estate investing requires planning and the allocation of money to protect and preserve your property investment in the long run.

Often sellers indicate that the property has been fully renovated and imply that the purchaser won't need to make any capital improvements for many years to come. But buildings age, and things wear and break — especially in rental properties. Allocate a portion of your income to reflect the fact that certain components of your property are deteriorating and will need to be replaced. Otherwise, you may find that your roof needs to be replaced and you don't have the funds to cover the expense.

Capital improvements are an essential component of the repositioning or renovation plans that lead to improved financial performance for investment real estate. As an investor, always consider properties that owners have neglected to properly maintain and upgrade. This category is one of the best target markets for investing, and your pro forma income and expenses should contain a realistic capital improvement budget.

Your pre-purchase due diligence should include a detailed walk-through of the property by a qualified contractor who can identify health and safety issues that should be addressed immediately — either during escrow by the seller or by you as the new owner. A leasing broker or someone knowledgeable about the competitive properties in the market should then compile a prioritized list of needed work and cost-effective upgrades that will position your property to deliver above-market returns.

Capital expenses are subjective. Be conservative and estimate toward the high side of a range. If you don't have to spend the funds, your real estate investment results are enhanced. But you don't want to plan on scrimping by not addressing needed repairs and replacements. Deferred maintenance is more costly to address in the future.

Surveying Lease Options

Leases for rental properties come in three basic forms:

- **Gross lease:** In a *gross lease,* the landlord pays for almost all of the operating expenses of the property.

- **Modified gross lease:** *Modified gross leases* pass some of the expenses of owning and operating the building directly to the tenants. Examples of modified gross leases include leases where the landlord pays all operating expenses except for certain items such as utilities, parking, or janitorial expenses.

- **Net lease:** The term *net lease* can have an unlimited range of variables but typically provides for the tenant to pay for the majority of the costs of operating the building, including property taxes, insurance, and maintenance costs.

You shouldn't include the cost of any tenant-paid services as an expense of the property. The leases for a commercial property can be gross leases, modified gross leases, or net leases, but residential properties are almost always leased on a gross basis, except utilities.

Comparing lease options

There are different thoughts about which type of lease is best. Many investors believe that net leases reduce the owner's management of the property, but this isn't necessarily true. The owner must still ensure that the property is properly maintained. One argument against net leases is that the tenant may skimp on the maintenance of the property, which is why you typically don't see net leases in residential properties.

 Modified gross leases in which the tenant pays for expenses that she can control are a good balance for all types of properties.

As the potential purchaser of a commercial property, carefully evaluate the leases and determine what operating expenses, if any, are paid by the tenants. You need to understand whether the property is using gross or net leases. Otherwise, you may be deceived regarding the actual NOI and cash flow that you will receive for the property.

Common area maintenance charges for commercial buildings

Costs in multitenant commercial buildings that are passed on to the tenant are called *common area maintenance (CAM) charges*. Paid proportionately by each tenant for the upkeep of areas designated for the use and benefit of all tenants, CAM charges include items such as parking lot maintenance, security, snow removal, and common area utilities. These charges are part of the tenant's rent and can be due in advance or paid in arrears; the lease establishes the terms. Some tenants negotiate that they don't have CAM charges. For accounting purposes, CAM charges are typically reflected in the cash flow as "CAM reimbursement" (see Table 8-1). Although they're indicated as an income item, they're essentially offsetting the corresponding expense items included in the property's operating expenses.

The most common method is to use an estimated annual budget for the property as a basis for the collection of a monthly CAM charge. At the end of a previously agreed upon time period (usually annually), you calculate the actual expenses incurred for the common area items and reconcile those against the amount paid by the tenants, billing the tenants for any shortfall or refunding any excess payments.

Basic Approaches to Value

Professional real estate appraisers traditionally use three basic valuation techniques to arrive at an accurate estimate of current value: the market data (or sales comparison) approach, the cost approach, and the income capitalization approach.

Typically, each valuation method arrives at a slightly to moderately different estimate of value, and the appraiser reconciles or weighs the different results based on the applicability or reliability in determining the final estimate of value. The appraiser's derived estimate of value may be greater or lower than the price a particular investor is willing to pay — the investment value. But lenders require appraisals to protect their position and show that the property has sufficient equity; if they're forced to foreclose and sell, they're less likely to suffer a loss.

Market data (sales comparison) approach

The *market data* or *sales comparison* approach takes the economic concept of substitution and applies it to real estate. In real estate, the *substitution principle* essentially states that the value of a given property should be approximately the same as a similar or comparable property that provides the same benefits. This method is very much like what you may do when purchasing a major item for your home — you compare similar items at various stores to assist you in determining what price to pay. Likewise, you don't want to pay more for one property than a similar property would cost.

The accuracy of the market data approach relies on a sufficient number of recent sales of comparable properties. This approach to valuation is primarily used for single-family homes, condos, and small apartment buildings because they're typically more plentiful and offer data from many recent sales.

Typically, appraisers look for at least three comparable properties in close proximity to the subject property. Of course, the usage and type of real estate should be the same, and a *good comp* is similar in age, size, features, amenities, and condition of the property. The timing of the sale is also important as well as the availability of seller financing.

Appraisers strive to find several comparable properties, but the reality is that every property is unique, and there are no *truly* identical sales or listings. So appraisers need to make either positive or negative adjustments to account for the differences. They then factor all of these variances into an adjustment to the price and then calculate an indicated value for the subject property.

Cost approach

The *cost* approach to real estate valuation is a variation on the market data approach that's useful when you don't have a lot of comparable sales data. It's more commonly used, and even the preferred method, for proposed construction, brand-new properties, and unique properties that typically don't generate an income (including schools, hospitals, public buildings, or places of worship).

_____

_____

_____

Real estate investors find that this method can be useful for establishing replacement cost. The replacement cost of a property can often be an indicator of barriers to entry that exist in the market. Owning superior location, well-maintained real estate in high demand with high barriers to entry for competing properties is one of the best ways to ensure the success of your real estate investments.

In determining valuation with the cost approach, each segment — the land and the improvements (buildings) — is evaluated separately.

Income capitalization approach

This method of valuation is primarily used for larger income-producing properties but can be useful for small income properties as well. (It's not used for valuing properties whose primary purpose isn't income producing.)

The *income capitalization* method is based on the principle that the greater the income generated, the more an investor is willing and able to pay for the property.

Our discussion of the income capitalization approach to valuation must start with the fundamental building block of determining value for this method — the *direct capitalization* or *IRV formula*. Here are the players in this formula:

- **Value (V):** With this method, you're looking to determine the value of a given property by examining the relationship between net operating income (NOI) and the capitalization rate (R).

- **Net operating income (NOI):** Check out the "Net Operating Income" section earlier in this chapter to determine this piece of the puzzle.

- **Capitalization rate (R):** Also called the *cap rate* and *overall rate*, this number is based on the market or the buyer's objectives. It's the rate of return most investors seek for similar properties in a similar market at a given time.

Put it all into equation form and you get

$$V \text{ (value)} = \frac{\text{NOI (Net operating income)}}{\text{R (Capitalization rate)}}$$

The cap rate can be subjective, but it's a measure of the risk-adjusted return a particular investor would expect to receive if he purchased a similar property at a similar price. Real estate brokers and agents often have information on current cap rates in the local market.

Reconciling the three results to arrive at a single value

An appraiser takes the numbers derived from the market data approach, the cost approach, and the income capitalization approach and *reconciles* them to determine a single estimate of market value at a specific time. However, the appraiser doesn't simply take an average of the three estimates of value because all three methods may not be equally valid or reliable for the subject property.

Rather, the reconciliation process takes into consideration the relative merits of each approach, with more weight given to the most applicable approach. For appraisals of income-producing real estate, appraisers and real estate investors generally rely most heavily on the income capitalization approach because the property is being acquired as an investment.

The appraisal process isn't an exact science, but the principles of valuation are important for real estate investors. You want to be able to estimate value so you don't overpay for a property. Your lender requires an appraisal to determine how much you can borrow. These same appraisal techniques can help you determine the appropriate asking price when you look to sell your real estate investment.

Deciding How Much to Pay

After you've done all of your research and calculations, you still need to determine whether a proposed property is a good opportunity — and at what price? You don't want to pay retail, but the typical properties you see are based on unrealistic representations by most sellers.

You want to buy when you project that the property has a strong likelihood of producing future increases in NOI and cash flow. Look for properties where your analysis shows that the income for the property can be increased or the expenses reduced.

In this chapter, we've covered NOI, cash flow, and the valuation techniques used by professionals. Using those techniques can help you to determine the maximum price you should pay for a property.

But sellers use similar techniques to set the maximum price they think they can get from the most generous buyer in the market. You need to understand how they may twist the facts to present their property in the best light. The following examples demonstrate how being able to properly value investment real estate before making a purchase offer is essential.

Examining the seller's rental rate and expense claims

Most sellers of investment properties claim that the rents are below market. Sellers may imply that instantly upon purchasing the building, the buyer will be able to enhance the value of her new investment property and improve her cash flow by merely (yet significantly) increasing rents.

Of course, you should be wondering: If I can make money by simply raising the rents, why doesn't the current owner increase the rents and then sell the building at a much higher price? After all, sellers know that buyers will base their offer on NOI. The answer is that they usually do raise rents before putting the property on the market. But sellers (and their real estate agents) still go ahead and claim that the buyer can raise the rents even more.

The same scenario is found with expenses. The seller typically cuts back on spending to show artificially low expenses, or claims that the buyer can cut expenses through an energy conservation program or some other seemingly sensible method. This mind-set assumes that the current owner hasn't taken advantage of legitimate ways to cut down on expenses.

Even if these claims are true, the buyer (you) shouldn't pay an inflated price based on the assumption of being able to make these changes because she'll have to pony up to make the changes herself. Implementing these strategies to generate higher income and lower expenses also takes many months.

Deciding which set of numbers to use

When you look at listings of properties for sale, you find that many sellers and their brokers or agents develop a pro forma, or future estimate, of the NOI. From this artificially high NOI, they then derive an above-market asking price for the property. In reality, the NOI drops if you lose some of your key tenants or are faced with a major unanticipated expense. This pro forma is an *estimate* of future operations of the property. The future is uncertain, so none of the numbers are truly right or wrong.

Although the IRV formula uses the future NOI, and the value of the building is determined based on those numbers, we suggest that you find a seller who calculated his asking price based on actual historical operating income and expenses. You want to anticipate the future and pay for the present. You need to set your offering price based on your own calculations as to the NOI you expect to earn in the year after your purchase.

The other key component to the IRV formula is the capitalization rate. If you lower the capitalization rate or required return, you can dramatically increase the value of the property. A lower rate of return is required when the risk associated with the cash flow of a property is lower. The risk is lower when the property is competitive with or superior to other comparable properties, has minimal deferred maintenance, and has solid tenants with leases in place that are at market. Your goal is to find properties that lack these characteristics but you can easily achieve with superior management.

9

Purchase Agreements

You and your real estate team log many hours in locating and valuing property. Then comes the moment when you must decide whether you want to try to buy a particular property or keep looking for a more attractive opportunity. In this chapter, we cover the all-important details of real estate investment contracts.

Contract Basics

The purchase and sale of real estate are always done in writing. The most critical document in any transaction is the sales contract, which is referred to as the *purchase agreement* in real estate transactions. After you've found a property that meets your investment goals, have your real estate agent prepare a real estate contract for presentation to the seller or her agent.

A real estate contract is a legally binding written agreement between two or more people regarding an exchange of some sort. These contracts are legally enforceable sets of promises that must be performed and that rely on the basics of contract law.

Bilateral versus unilateral contracts

Real estate contracts can be either bilateral or unilateral:

- **Bilateral:** Most real estate contracts are *bilateral*, meaning that each party to the contract promises to provide some *consideration* (something of value) and adhere to the terms of the contract. For example, the seller agrees to give the buyer title to the property in exchange for cash and/or a *promissory note* (a written document promising to pay the holder of the note a certain sum of money at some given time in the future).

- **Unilateral:** A unilateral contract is a one-sided agreement in which only one party promises to do something. An example is an *option agreement* in which the seller *(optionor)* gives a potential buyer *(optionee)* an unconditional purchase option for a certain period of time. The option is enforceable only by the optionee. If the option isn't properly exercised, the optionor's obligation and the optionee's rights expire.

Elements of a contract

A *legally binding* contract is valid because it contains all of the necessary elements that make it legally enforceable. In the following list, we outline the basic elements of a legally binding and enforceable real estate contract. The terms may sound a bit technical, but you need to be familiar with them.

- **Legally competent parties:** Every party to the transaction must have *legal capacity,* which is defined as being of legal age (18 in most states) and having the mental capacity to understand the consequences of its actions.

- **An offer:** An *offer* to purchase real estate is a written communication to the current owner of the buyer's willingness to purchase a specific property at the terms indicated. The seller can continue to market the property while considering the offer. Unless an expiration clause is included, an offer may be accepted by the seller at any time before it's rescinded by the buyer.

Virtually all offers have a specific expiration time. You want to allow the seller a reasonable time to receive, consider, and evaluate your offer, but enforce the expiration clause to minimize the seller from using the offer as a negotiating tool with other interested parties, shopping your offer around, or trying to entice another buyer to raise her offer.

- **Acceptance:** *Acceptance* is a positive written response in a timely manner to the exact terms of an offer. Acceptance legally requires that the buyer must be given legal notice of the acceptance. Commonly, the seller doesn't accept the offer as presented but proposes changes in the terms or conditions — which is a *counteroffer.*

- **Counteroffer:** This is legally a new offer; the original offer is rejected and is void. Counteroffers can go back and forth until both buyer and seller have agreed and the final accepted offer becomes the binding agreement between the parties. Just like offers, counteroffers must be in writing and can be rescinded at any time before acceptance.

- **Consideration:** *Consideration* is the exchange aspect of the deal: The buyer offers payment of money or something of value to the seller, who agrees to give over ownership of the property in return. A real estate contract isn't binding if each party doesn't offer at least some consideration to the other party.

- **Clearly and uniquely identified property:** This identification is required so there's no uncertainty about precisely which property is being sold and transferred to the buyer. Typically, a legal description of the property is used.

- **Legal purpose:** The real estate contract must be for a legal purpose and can't be for an illegal act or an act so immoral that it's against public policy.

- **Written contract:** A written contract is required for all enforceable transfers of real estate. All terms and conditions of the purchase agreement or sales contract must be set forth in writing, even for minor items that may not seem consequential. Generally, the written contract helps ensure that there is no confusion about what is included in the sale. For example, if you want to make sure that the supplies in the maintenance shop for a commercial or apartment building are included and not taken before the sale, you must specify it in the contract. If something isn't in writing, it's not part of the contract.

Agreements for the sale of real estate must be in writing or they're unenforceable. *Never* make an oral agreement of any type regarding real estate no matter how convenient, expedient, or reasonable it may seem at the time. The Statute of Frauds is a legal concept that requires all transfers of real estate to be in writing to be enforceable in a court of law.

A failure to meet all of these essential elements can lead to the contract being declared void. A void contract has no legal force or effect and is unenforceable in a court of law.

Besides all the legal elements, real estate sales contracts specify the sale price and the terms and conditions as well as any contingencies (see the "Contingencies" section later in the chapter). The contract must be signed and include a standard statement that "time is of the essence," which ensures that all dates and times of day noted in the contract can't be ignored by any of the parties without the written consent of the other party; otherwise, there is a breach of the contract. If the contract is breached, the other party may be entitled to monetary damages or can sue to force the seller to complete the sale.

Key Provisions in the Purchase Agreement

The purchase agreement is the legal document that outlines the details of the transaction for your proposed purchase of the subject property. Depending on where you live, there are other terms for a contract for the purchase of real estate, such as a *sales contract,* an *offer to purchase,* a *contract of purchase and sale,* an *earnest money agreement,* and a *deposit receipt.*

No matter what you call it, the purchase agreement is the most important document in the sale of real estate. It includes the basic info — the names of the sellers and buyers, a description of the property, and the proposed financing terms — and indicates how much you pay, when you pay, the terms and conditions that must be met to close the transaction, and the conditions under which the agreement can be canceled and the buyer's deposit returned.

Go over the purchase agreement form in detail with your real estate broker or agent and carefully consider the terms that you want to offer in each paragraph. Don't leave any blank spaces, and have your attorney mark through any clauses that you feel aren't appropriate. Just because a certain clause is preprinted doesn't mean you can't cross it out or modify the language to suit your needs. Make sure you clearly initial any changes and require the other party to also initial every single change and the bottom of each page to ensure that you agreed on the specific terms.

Some of the terms are at your discretion, but your real estate agent can advise you as to the local custom and practice concerning issues such as the standard for earnest money deposits (see the next section) or the length of contingency periods for inspections of the property, books, and records. Your agent can also inform you about local standards for prorating the closing agent costs and the other miscellaneous costs of the transaction.

The following sections cover other key provisions you should carefully evaluate because you must make many decisions about your offer before the purchase agreement is ready for your signature.

Earnest money deposit

Right after the purchase price, one of the most important terms that can set the tone for further negotiations is the amount of the earnest money deposit you're willing to submit with your purchase offer. The *earnest money deposit* is usually fully refundable for a defined time period. Your deposit is held in trust by either the seller's agent or a title or escrow company. Never make an earnest money deposit payable directly to the seller.

The purpose of the deposit is to show good faith by the buyer and the intention to follow through with the terms of the purchase agreement. The amount of the deposit varies in different areas depending on local custom or the specific needs of a particular transaction. Also, depending on state law, the earnest money deposit may or may not go into an interest-bearing account.

When determining the earnest money deposit, remember that if you don't live up to the agreement or don't cancel it within the allowed time frames, you forfeit the deposit to the seller. The forfeiture of the earnest money deposit for nonperformance is called *liquidated damages,* which is essentially the payment for any and all damages incurred by the seller as a result of your not completing the purchase as proposed. Under the terms of most purchase agreements, a seller who keeps the earnest money deposit can't sue for any further damages.

To avoid any expensive lessons about earnest money, follow this advice:

- As a buyer, make sure you know the exact date on which your earnest money *goes hard*, which is the real estate industry term meaning it's nonrefundable and passes to the seller regardless of whether you complete the purchase of the property.

- Don't wait until the last few days to cancel your purchase agreement. If you're still unsure of your interest or ability to complete the transaction as proposed, send a written cancellation of the purchase agreement and then try to negotiate additional time, while spelling out in detail what your concerns are and why you need more time.

- Both buyer and seller must agree to any changes in writing. Never rely on any verbal representations as to any extensions or changes of terms or conditions.

Assigning your rights

Many purchase agreements specifically include a clause giving the buyer the ability to assign his interests to another party.

Assignment is the transfer of the right or duties under a real estate contract by the buyer to a third party. This is an extremely important clause for buyers, and we strongly encourage you to include the right to assign the contract as a term of your purchase offer. In the contract, simply include the language "or assignee" after the name of the legal entity indicated as the purchaser. If the preprinted purchase offer has a clause that prohibits assignment, you need to cross out that language and have both parties initial the change.

The ability to assign your interests in a purchase agreement can be a lifesaver. Many savvy investors have gotten into a real estate transaction in which the due diligence time frames have passed and their earnest money is at risk — and they're unable or unwilling to complete the transaction. This situation typically happens because the buyer has second thoughts, doesn't have enough money to close, finds a better deal, or doesn't have the capability to handle the problems with the property. In this scenario, an assignment would allow the buyer to potentially recover his earnest money deposit or even his due diligence costs from another interested buyer rather than walk away and let the seller take the earnest money (and then turn around and sell the property to another party). The buyer who has the property under contract controls the property and can make a deal with other parties.

The closing date

An important term of your purchase offer is the proposed closing date for the transaction, which determines the anticipated escrow period (see Chapter 10 for escrow information). The length of the escrow period is a matter of negotiation between the buyer and seller, with consideration given to the length of time needed to obtain financing and the amount and complexity of due diligence necessary to complete the sale.

Of course, the seller is usually interested in selling the property as soon as possible and wants a short escrow period and a fixed closing date; the buyer generally wants as much time as the seller will allow, some flexibility on the closing date, and the unilateral right to close the transaction earlier if he's completed his work.

The more time for the buyer, the better opportunity he has to make sure he's not making a mistake — and the seller knows that. But, the seller also knows that many buyers use an extended due diligence period to find problems with the property and try to wear down the seller into granting concessions or lowering the purchase price.

Ultimately, what you agree on in the purchase agreement is legally binding, but it's really just an estimated closing date because so many moving parts can affect when you close the sale. The closing date should be met unless both parties agree to an extension with a written addendum or escrow instruction (see "Ironing out straggling issues" later in the chapter).

Contingencies

A *contingency* in a real estate purchase agreement is simply a condition that must be fulfilled or an event that may or may not happen before a contract becomes firm and binding. Contingencies can be for the benefit of either the seller or the buyer; if the contingencies aren't met, the deal doesn't go through. The seller of an estate property, for example, may require a contingency that the probate court approves the sale. Buyers often have contingencies for financing, physical inspections, the review of the current tenant leases and service contracts that will run with the property, and other items. Naturally, sellers attempt to eliminate unreasonable contingencies.

Contingencies are escape clauses that can protect the buyer from purchasing a property that doesn't meet his needs. Without contingencies, purchasing a property would be extremely risky because you'd have to be sure that you had all of the financing in place and that the property was in good condition, met your needs, and the terms and conditions were acceptable before you even made the offer. Few buyers would be willing to do this, or they'd do it but discount their offer to account for the additional risk.

The terms of most purchase agreements provide that by certain defined dates, all of the contingencies must be resolved one way or another by the *beneficiary*, or party that stands to gain from the contingency. After it's in place, a contingency has one of three outcomes:

- **Contingencies can be satisfied.** This means that the pending sale is no longer subject to cancellation or modification for that particular item.

- **The beneficiary of the contingency can unilaterally agree to waive or remove the contingency.**

- **A contingency can be rejected or fail.** The beneficiary of the contingency is then no longer obligated to perform under the contract.

Although the list varies depending on the property type, size, and location, here are contingency clauses that we recommend:

- **Marketable title:** Obtain a preliminary title report with full and complete copies of each and every exception and have your attorney review these documents.

- **Financing:** Outline the specific terms (type of loan and maximum acceptable interest rate) of a new loan required to complete the purchase.

- **Appraisal:** This condition demands that an independent professional appraisal of the property arrives at a value equal to or greater than the proposed purchase price. This requirement may be a necessary part of the financing or simply a safeguard to prevent you from overpaying for the property.

- **Physical inspection:** Most purchase agreements include an inspection clause mandating that you have unlimited access to the property for a certain amount of time to inspect the interior and exterior of the property.

- **Books and records inspection:** If you're purchasing a large residential or commercial property, another important contingency is the opportunity to review and inspect the income and expense statements and the leases. Ask for a copy of the seller's Schedule E (filed with the IRS) to ensure that the income and expenses for the property are consistent with what the seller has been reporting.

- **ALTA property survey:** This survey shows the property boundaries or parcel map along with the site plan for all existing improvements, plus any easements and restrictions.

- **Contracts:** Make sure you receive copies of all service agreements and contracts currently in place at the property. Ideally, the seller should be required to cancel or terminate all nonessential contracts (unless they're especially attractive in the current market conditions) at the close of escrow so you have the option of bringing in your own preferred vendors.

Ironing out straggling issues

In addition to the contingency clauses, many buyers negotiate a separate clause giving them the unilateral right to extend the closing date under certain conditions. Be sure that all parties agree to any such extension in writing before the closing date indicated in the purchase agreement to avoid any potential disputes.

Be sure that your purchase agreement clearly indicates what personal property is included. The personal property can be a significant factor in large apartment buildings because it can include the appliances and window coverings, plus common area furnishings and fixtures, as well as parts, materials, and supplies for future maintenance and repairs.

Depending on your plans for the property, you may want the property transferred with or without tenants. If the tenants aren't on valid and enforceable long-term leases, and you can increase the property value by renovation and gaining new tenants, requiring the seller to deliver the property vacant and what's called *broom clean* (free of debris, dirt, personal property, furniture, and so on) at the close of escrow can be prudent. This is also true if you buy a seller-occupied property. Either include a clause requiring that the seller vacates prior to the close of escrow, or negotiate a lease for continued tenancy at mutually agreeable terms.

_____

_____

_____

The Purchase Agreement

After you and your agent are comfortable with the purchase agreement you've prepared, your agent will present your agreement to the seller's agent.

Your offer should include a set time limit for response. Depending on the type of property and the size of the transaction, give the seller 24 to 72 hours from when you believe that he will first receive your offer to respond to the offer. The larger and more complicated the transaction, the more time the seller needs to evaluate your offer. The seller can accept your offer as presented, respond with a counteroffer, reject the offer, or simply let it expire. After your offer for the property is accepted, you control the property and have it *under contract.*

10

Escrow, Due Diligence, and Property Inspections

Your work as a buyer is just beginning when you have an accepted offer for your proposed acquisition, the property is under contract, and an escrow account has been opened. You control the property and can begin to determine whether the seller has accurately represented it.

This is when the formal due diligence period begins. *Due diligence* is the pre-escrow process you (or your representatives) perform to investigate the property's physical and fiscal condition.

Complete the transaction only if the property physically and fiscally meets your needs and the financing is satisfactory. But the property may still be worth pursuing if the seller is willing to correct deficiencies or give you a monetary credit to cover your costs to complete the necessary work yourself.

In this chapter, we focus on some of the important issues in opening an escrow, conducting formal due diligence, performing property inspections, and handling credits in escrow.

Opening Escrow

Escrow is a method of completing a real estate transaction in which a disinterested third party acts as the intermediary to coordinate the closing activities. The first step after the buyer and the seller sign the purchase agreement is for the *earnest money* funds (the money you give the seller upfront as partial payment and confirmation of your good faith and intent to close the deal) to be deposited with the escrow holder and put in an escrow account in the buyer's name.

A real estate transaction for even small investment properties can be complicated because the buyer and seller have different interests that need to be fairly represented. The escrow holder acts as a neutral third party who handles the details of the transaction and often serves as the referee when disagreements develop between buyer and seller.

An escrow officer at an escrow company or a title company can handle escrow. Although escrow officers handle most escrows, in some areas of the country, attorneys act as the intermediary throughout the transaction. We refer to escrow officers, escrow agents, and real estate attorneys who handle the closing simply as *escrow officers* throughout this chapter.

Escrow instructions

The escrow officer prepares the escrow instructions that guide the transaction between the parties. The *escrow instructions* are derived from the specific terms found in the purchase agreement and in any other written documents mutually agreed upon by both the buyer and seller.

The escrow instructions are critical. To minimize surprises, carefully review the instructions before you sign them because that's the document that the escrow holder relies on to determine what to do in the event of a dispute. Unless allowed in the escrow instructions, the escrow officer can't make any changes or respond to any requests without a written agreement signed by all parties.

The escrow officer only performs items that are mutually agreed upon, in writing, by both the buyer and the seller. If the escrow officer receives conflicting information or requests, nothing happens until all parties reach an agreement or obtain a court order instructing the escrow officer. If something isn't allowed in the escrow instructions, both the seller and the buyer must present a fully executed change order to the escrow officer modifying the agreement. In other words, make sure the escrow instructions meet your expectations before you sign them.

Preliminary title report

Soon after the escrow instructions have been signed, your title company should send you a copy of the preliminary title report (or *prelim*). Have this extremely important document reviewed by an attorney unless you have a lot of personal experience and the prelim contains relatively few indicated items.

The preliminary title report indicates the current legal owner of the property and any mortgage liens, unpaid income tax liens, property tax liens, judgment liens, or other recorded encumbrances against the property. It also shows any easements, restrictions, or third-party interests that limit your use of the property such as the Covenants, Conditions, and Restrictions (C, C, and Rs) commonly found with planned unit developments, community associations, or condominiums.

_____

_____

_____

Obtain and review copies of the detailed backup materials for each item so you know exactly what's encumbering the property. The approval of the preliminary title report by the buyer is one of the basic contingencies in most real estate transactions. You have the right (subject to certain time limitations) to cancel the purchase if the preliminary title report contains unacceptable items. Of course, you can also require the seller to have unacceptable items removed or renegotiate the price and terms in order to continue with the transaction.

Removing contingencies

As we discuss in Chapter 9, the purchase agreement should contain several contingencies that allow the buyer and seller the opportunity to cancel the transaction if certain items aren't satisfactory. It's the escrow officer's job to track these contingencies and receive and follow the instructions from the buyer and seller.

Contingencies are critical elements that can make or break a transaction. The purchase agreement and escrow instructions usually contain deadlines — the parties have certain rights pertaining to contingencies for a limited period of time. For example, the physical inspection contingency may provide only ten days to make the inspection; after that the contingency is considered approved (or satisfied), and the seller has the legal right to refuse access for a physical inspection.

The holder of the contingency option must notify the escrow officer at once if the contingency is rejected or fails. Also, it isn't the escrow officer's responsibility to attempt to negotiate or mediate a resolution of any rejected contingencies or other deal-threatening issues that arise during the escrow. It's up to the buyer and seller and their respective agents to come up with solutions and keep the deal alive.

Estimated closing date

After all of the buyer's and seller's contingencies pertaining to items such as the financing, appraisal, books and records, and the physical inspection have been met or waived, the escrow officer advises the parties of the estimated closing date for the transaction.

When buying real estate, the process generally takes longer than planned. Therefore, if you're intent on keeping your efforts to purchase your investment property from going awry because of unanticipated delays, make provisions upfront that provide the additional time to properly close the transaction. These provisions typically take the form of closing extension options and may involve an additional payment to the seller to cover their continued costs of ownership or an increase in the amount of funds paid by the buyer to show good faith. Often, you have an agreement to release some or all of the earnest money or down payment to the seller as a nonrefundable payment.

This suggestion doesn't mean that the escrow should be allowed to drag on for months, but the more costly the property in escrow, the more likely you are to encounter unexpected challenges in satisfying or removing contingencies. Nonresidential property transactions tend to take longer to complete because the leases are more complicated to analyze and the buyer wants *estoppel certificates* (a legal document completed by the tenant that outlines the basic terms of his lease agreement and certifies that the lease is valid without any breaches by either the tenant or the landlord at the time it's executed) from each tenant.

_____

_____

_____

No matter the size of your deal, negotiate the right to extend escrow. Some local Realtor boards have developed a separate addendum that provides for extensions under certain conditions to enhance the likelihood of the transaction's completion. These extensions usually provide for an initial 14-day extension at no cost if the closing is delayed due to issues beyond the buyer's control. However, additional extensions are typically only allowed if the buyer compensates the seller for the equivalent of the seller's mortgage payment and/or her lost rental income if the property is vacant.

Due Diligence

The *due diligence period* (the time period between the acceptance of an offer and the close of escrow or completion of the sale) is the time to ask the tough questions. Don't be shy. Talk to the tenants, the neighbors, any homeowners or commercial association, governmental agencies, and the contractors or suppliers to the property, and be sure you know what you're getting.

Communicate regularly and work closely with the seller and his representatives, but only rely on information provided in writing. This time period may be your best or only opportunity to seek adjustments if important issues have been represented inaccurately. After the property sale is completed, it's too late to ask the seller to fix the leaky roof unless she has engaged in an intentional effort to cover up the property's true condition. Your remedies may only be in court, which can be costly and reserved for the most serious or expensive issues.

Practical examples of due diligence include collecting economic data about the region and neighborhood, calling competitive properties for current market rental rates and concessions, verifying the accuracy of the financial information and leases presented by the seller, and conducting a thorough inspection of the property by a licensed general contractor or property inspector. Although you may have completed some of these items before presenting your initial offer, some of the information may only become apparent from a review of the seller's books and records plus the unlimited access to the property that's generally only available during the formal due diligence.

Don't underestimate the importance of this step — this review of the books and records, along with the physical inspection, reveals the actual operations of the property and allows you to determine whether the property is suitable, fairly priced, and meets your financial goals. The due diligence period is your last chance to decide whether you should complete the transaction or cancel the escrow, get your money back, and search for a new possible acquisition.

Reviewing the books and records

Although savvy real estate investors conduct pre-offer due diligence and often receive a copy of a pro forma operating statement, you likely won't have an opportunity to review the books and records until you're formally under contract and in the due diligence period. Here are some things to make sure you have on hand *before* the deal is final:

- **Seller-verified income and expense statement for at least the past 12 months:** The actual income and expense history reveals any surprises that may not have been obvious from the pro forma statement you received from the seller. The best source of this information is the seller's Schedule E from her federal income tax return — you can be fairly sure that she's unlikely to overstate income or understate expenses to the IRS!

This statement also gives you a good idea of where to look for opportunities to improve on the financial performance of the property.

- **Seller-verified rent roll:** A *rent roll* is a list of all rental units with the tenant name, move-in date, lease expiration date, current and market rent, and the security deposit. Also, get a seller statement that no undisclosed verbal agreements, concessions, or side agreements have been made with any tenant regarding the rent, security deposits, payment of the utilities, or any other aspects of the financial terms of the lease or rental agreement.

- **Seller-verified list of all tenant security deposits on hand:** When acquiring a new rental property, follow state or local laws in properly handling the tenant's security deposit. Many state laws require the seller and/or purchaser of a rental property to advise the tenants in writing of the status of their deposit. The law usually gives the seller the right to either return the deposit to the tenant or transfer it to the new owner.

  If the seller refunds the security deposits, you have the challenge of collecting deposits from tenants already in possession of the rental unit or suite, which is never easy. For this reason, strongly urge the seller to provide you a credit for the full amount of the security deposits on hand in escrow and have each tenant agree in writing to the amount of the security deposit transferred during the sale. This strategy streamlines the process and prevents you from having to recollect security deposits from current tenants. To avoid problems at the time of move-out, send your tenant a letter confirming the security deposit amount.

- **Copies of the entire tenant file of each current tenant:** Make sure you have the rental application, current and past leases or rental agreements, all legal notices, maintenance work orders, and correspondence for every tenant. Also, insist that the seller advise you in writing about any pending legal action involving your tenant's occupancy.

- **Copies of every service agreement or contract:** Review all current contractors and service providers the current owner uses. If you plan to terminate the services of a contractor or service provider, the seller may be willing to send a written conditional notice of termination indicating that, if the property sells as planned, that contractor's services will no longer be needed as of the close of escrow. You can then find new contractors or maybe even renegotiate better terms with the current company.

- **Copies of all required governmental licenses and permits:** In many areas, rental property owners are now required to have business licenses, certificates, or permits. Contact the appropriate governmental office in writing and make sure they're properly notified of the change in ownership and/or billing address. Often these governmental entities have stiff penalties if you fail to notify them of a change in ownership in a timely manner. And they'll eventually discover the change in ownership because they usually monitor the local recording of deeds and receive notification of changes in billing responsibility from local utility companies. Make sure you have current copies of all state and local rental laws and ordinances that affect your rental property.

- **Comprehensive list of all personal property included in the purchase:** This inventory may include appliances, equipment, and supplies owned by the current property owner. *Remember:* Don't assume anything is included in the sale unless you have it in writing.

- **Copies of the latest utility billing:** Get all of the account and payment information for every utility provider. Before the close of escrow, contact each company and arrange for the transfer of utilities or a change in the billing responsibility as of the estimated escrow closing date. If provided with sufficient advance notice, many utility companies can have the meters read and/ or the billing cutoff coincide with the close of escrow, preventing the need to prorate any of the utility billings between the owners.

  Also find out whether the seller has any deposits on hand with the utility company and whether you need to place a deposit for service. You may be able to simply handle the transfer of the deposit through escrow with a written deposit transfer acknowledgment from the utility.

- **Copy of the seller's current insurance policy (if available) and the loss history:** One of the most important steps in the takeover of your new rental property is securing insurance coverage. Make sure you have the proper insurance policy in place at the time that you legally become the new owner. Most lenders won't fund your loan until they have written evidence that the property is adequately insured. Although the seller's policy can't protect you, request a copy of her policy or declaration of coverage and the loss history; this information can be helpful to your insurance broker or agent when analyzing the property to determine the proper coverage.

When you receive this information, verify the accuracy of all records. Most sellers are honest and don't intentionally withhold information or fail to disclose important facts, but the old adage "buyer beware" is particularly true in the purchase of rental real estate. Questions and issues that are resolved at this time can eliminate unpleasant and contentious disagreements with your tenants in the future. The takeover of your new rental property can be chaotic, but don't fall into the trap of just verbally verifying the facts. Verify all information in writing and set up a detailed filing system for your new property. Ultimately, the best proof of the expenses is to insist on receiving copies of last year's invoices to verify operating costs such as utilities.

Inspecting the property

The condition of a property directly affects its value. The prudent real estate investor always insists on a thorough physical inspection before purchasing an investment property even if the property is brand-new.

A new investment property may look good on paper, and your pre-offer due diligence may reveal no legal or financial issues or concerns. But your investment is only as good as the weakest link, and a physically troubled property is never a good investment (unless you're buying the property for the land and plan to demolish the current buildings).

You're probably making one of the biggest financial purchases and commitments of your life. Though real estate investors by nature tend to be frugal, never try to save money by forgoing a proper physical inspection by qualified experts. Unless you have extensive experience as a builder and contractor, you probably have no idea what you're getting into when it comes to evaluating the condition of most building systems.

An inspection usually pays for itself. Inevitably, you're going to find items that the seller needs to correct that are greater in value or cost to repair than the nominal sum you spend on the inspection.

The best result is if the inspection reveals no problems. Although you've spent money, it's a great relief to know that your property (at least at the time of the inspection) is in good condition.

Virtually all real estate purchase contracts provide that the transaction can be canceled without penalty or loss of the earnest money deposit if the buyer's physical inspection isn't satisfactory. But often, additional negotiations between the buyer and seller result. It's this competently prepared written inspection report that provides the information you need and serves as the basis to go back and ask the property seller to fix the problems or reduce the property's purchase price (see the "Negotiating Credits in Escrow" section later in the chapter).

Disclosure requirements

With purchases of a residential rental property with four or fewer units, many states have seller *disclosure requirements:* Sellers must provide the buyer with a written transfer disclosure statement that outlines all known structural and mechanical deficiencies. In many areas, sellers must also complete a comprehensive information questionnaire. The agents, if any, for both parties also complete a written disclosure indicating that they've made a reasonably diligent visual inspection of the interior and exterior of the property.

However, investors purchasing residential investment properties with five or more units or any type of commercial property typically don't have the same legislative protections. This discrepancy is based on the premise that these buyers and sellers and their respective agents are more sophisticated and don't need the mandatory protections of a formal written *transfer disclosure statement* (commonly abbreviated as *TDS form*).

Whether the transfer disclosure statement form is legally required or not, sellers in some states still have a legal duty to disclose any and all material facts that could impact the value or intended use of the property.

The as-is gambit

Some sellers attempt to avoid any disclosures by proposing that their property is being sold to you strictly on an as-is and where-is basis. The theory is that an as-is sale means the seller isn't required to correct any deficiencies in the property before the completion of the sale, and they're not responsible for any issues that arise after the sale. They erroneously believe that such terms are legally enforceable under all conditions and act as a blanket disclaimer against claims of misrepresentation, fraud, or negligence. However, in most areas of the country, the as-is strategy only offers minimal protection to the seller.

Be extremely careful if considering the purchase of a property offered on an as-is basis. An as-is property is a major red flag; you should sincerely consider whether it's worth the increased risk. Although the seller may simply be following the ill-advised recommendations of the broker or seminar guru, some sellers are dishonest and hide significant issues that reduce the property's true value. A property offered on an as-is basis significantly below the expected market value is rarely a good deal.

Types of inspections

If you can get full access to the property, conduct your own brief physical exterior and interior inspection before making your offer. This initial overview doesn't cost anything other than your time and keeps you from wasting further time on properties that have obvious major problems. But this walk-through is no substitute for a professional inspection.

Don't rush the inspection process. The seller must give you complete and unfettered access to the entire property. Don't agree to any unreasonable time or access limitations. We've seen sneaky sellers who unrealistically limit access to the property, particularly if it's occupied. Make sure the tenants have been properly notified, as required by law and/or their lease agreements, with a liberal access time period so you can thoroughly conduct all of your inspections without interference or interruptions.

There are generally three types of professional inspections performed during the due diligence period while your property is in escrow, and we cover them in the following sections.

Physical or structural inspection

Naturally, you as the buyer want to have all of the physical aspects of the structures on your property inspected. However, your lender may also require you to pay for a separate physical assessment or property inspection report by a firm of its choice. This stipulation is typical only for medium to large residential and commercial types of properties.

Pest control and property damage

Pest control firms are the natural choice for this type of inspection, but what they inspect is actually more than just infestations by termites, bedbugs, carpenter ants, powder post beetles, and other wood-destroying insects. A thorough pest control and property damage inspection also looks at property damage caused by organisms that infect and incessantly break down and destroy wood and other building materials. These conditions are commonly referred to as *dry rot,* but ironically they're actually a fungus that requires moisture to flourish.

The report you receive from your pest control and property damage inspector usually includes a simple diagram of the property with notations as to the location of certain conditions noted. Some require attention immediately; others are simply areas to watch in the future.

Environmental issues

For commercial and residential rental investment properties with five or more units, a lender usually requires a *phase I environmental report,* which reviews the property records for the site, including all prior owners and uses of the property and aerial photographs, and may include a site visit, but no testing.

Review the report prepared for the lender at your expense, and make sure there are no surprises. Only purchase properties if they have a clear environmental report, regardless of the price. The downside of environmentally challenged properties is so significant that you should obtain the phase I environmental report even if you're purchasing the property for cash.

Most properties don't have problems, and the phase I report is all that is required. However, a negative phase I report makes further investigation and remediation necessary. Problems found in the phase I report can be expensive and cause delays of several weeks or even months while additional testing and analysis takes place, a phase II environmental assessment report is prepared, and contractors complete the required work per the specifications outlined by the environmental engineers and consultants.

Have an environmental engineer check drains and pipes that connect to the storm drain system or sewer to ensure that toxic or hazardous materials haven't been disposed of through your proposed property. If the EPA or comparable state agency later determines that the source of the contaminants was your property, you could face a budget-busting cleanup bill. The governmental agencies don't care that these violations occurred under prior ownership.

Lenders are extremely concerned about making a loan on a property with the potential for environmental hazards. They know that many buyers would simply walk away from the property and leave them with the devastating cost of cleaning up the property. That's why most lenders now require buyers to remain personally responsible for environmental issues even if the loan is *nonrecourse* (the lender can only foreclose on the underlying property in the event of a default). This provision is commonly referred to as a *carve-out* and is designed to protect the lender from owners who may be tempted to bail out and leave the lender on the hook for a contaminated property.

Qualifying the inspectors

Just like selecting the closing agent, many real estate investors pick inspectors as an afterthought or simply take the recommendation of their real estate agent. But inspect the property inspectors before you hire one. As with other service professionals, interview a few inspectors before making your selection. You may find that they don't all share the same experience, qualifications, and ethical standards.

_____

_____

_____

The inspection is a unique opportunity for most property owners and, because you're paying, we strongly recommend that you join the inspector while he's assessing your proposed purchase. What you learn can be invaluable and may pay dividends throughout your entire ownership. When an unscrupulous contractor later tries to tell you that you need to completely replumb your property, you can tell him to get lost if your property inspection revealed only isolated problems that can be resolved inexpensively.

Only consider full-time, professional inspectors. Hire an inspector who performs at least 100 comprehensive inspections per year and carries errors and omissions insurance. Such coverage isn't cheap and is another key indicator that the person is working full time in the field and is participating in ongoing continuing education.

The inspection report must be written, and to avoid surprises, request a sample of one of the recent inspection reports that have been prepared for a comparable property. This simple request may eliminate several potential inspectors but is essential so you can see whether an inspector is qualified and how detailed a report he will prepare for you.

The advent of digital photography is a boon to property inspectors and makes their sometimes mundane and difficult-to-understand reports come to life. Select a technologically savvy inspector and require her to electronically send you her report, including digital photos documenting all of the conditions noted. With the report in the electronic realm, it's a simple process to email this information as needed.

Although the cost of the inspection should be set in advance, the price should be a secondary concern because inspection fees often pay for themselves. Just like many other professional services, there is a direct correlation between the pricing of your inspection and the amount of time the inspector takes to conduct the inspection and then prepare the report.

Finally, require the finalists to provide the names and phone numbers of at least ten people who used the company's services within the past six months. Randomly call and make sure that these clients were satisfied and that the inspector acted professionally and ethically.

Negotiating Credits in Escrow

Most purchase agreements require the seller to deliver the property in good physical condition with all basic systems in operational order unless otherwise indicated. But the inspection process often reveals deficiencies that need to be corrected.

With your inspection reports in hand, preferably with digital photos, you're prepared to contact the seller's representative(s) and arrange for the seller to correct the noted items at his expense. The seller may debate some of the items and claim that the property is being sold as-is even if he didn't previously indicate any such thing. Be prepared to refer him to the warranty of condition clause in your copy of the purchase agreement; hopefully he takes care of the problems without further delay.

Some sellers and buyers prefer to handle deficiencies through a monetary credit in escrow in favor of the buyer so the buyer can make the needed repairs on his own. This route is particularly beneficial if you plan on making significant renovations to the property or the item is one of a personal nature — like the type and color of replacement carpet for a rental house. In that case, giving you a credit that you can use to pick the type, grade, and color of carpeting or even an entirely different type of floor covering that suits your needs is a sensible approach. The seller shouldn't be concerned as long as the amount is equal to or less than his cost to do the work; plus, the seller doesn't have the hassle of coordinating the work or making payments.

A buyer who receives a credit in escrow is often anxious to get started on making improvements to get the property in rent-ready condition immediately upon the close of escrow. Although tempting, you should be wary of making significant renovation or repairs to the property before the close of escrow. If the sale of the property doesn't go through, you may have spent considerable sums to upgrade the seller's property without any recourse.

11

Closing the Transaction

The closing of escrow is the consummation of the real estate transaction and the goal of the buyer, the seller, the brokers, and all the other professionals who were part of the effort. It's the culmination of numerous acts and negotiation right up until the last moment. The closing of escrow occurs only when all conditions of the escrow instructions and purchase agreement are fulfilled, including any funding of the loan. Quite a few details must come together before the escrow officer can close the transaction and record the deed.

In this chapter, we cover last-minute problems that may arise, closing the transaction, and taking over the property.

Complications

A few fundamental items and details need to be addressed as you wind down the escrow before you can call the property your own. Snags are still possible, so keep an eye out for the following:

- **Lender requests:** You need to make sure you're in contact with your lender to avoid any last-minute snafus. Lenders are notorious for needing just one more signature or asking questions at the last minute about the source of your down payment. These questions aren't as random as they may seem and are usually brought up by the loan committee or final person who must sign off on your loan.

- **Document errors:** Don't assume the documents are correct. They're prepared by people who may not be careful or who even cut and paste from documents used in prior escrows that have nothing to do with your transaction.

- **Availability of parties and busy periods:** You need to be available to review and sign the loan documents, so let the lender or your mortgage broker know if you're planning any trips around closing time. And during certain times of the year, like December holidays, spring break season, and holiday weekends, things just take a lot longer.

Eleventh-hour issues are bound to arise, so don't leave important details to the last minute or you may struggle to make deadlines, particularly if there is a penalty clause to extend your escrow. You can almost guarantee lost documents and other unexplained communication breakdowns that occur anytime you have so many moving parts. Anticipate logistical delays and allow time for everything to take twice as long as it should.

Estimated Closing Statement

Several days before the projected date for the close of your escrow, both the buyer and the seller receive a copy of the estimated closing statement with the various charges. You may receive this statement at the time you sign some or all of the documents, or it may be sent to you separately. Receiving this statement is an important step because it gives you time to raise any issues or concerns if you feel an error has been made.

The estimated amounts can, and usually do, change slightly. Often the escrow officer or closing agent estimates these expenses a little on the high side because any shortage of funds prevents the escrow from closing, but any overage can easily be credited or refunded back to the buyer or seller.

The buyer should pay particular attention to the estimated closing statement because it indicates the funds expected to be received from the lender. It also indicates the amount of cash that the buyer needs to deposit in the form of a wire transfer, cashier's check, or other certified funds. The buyer must provide these *good funds* in plenty of time for the escrow to close.

Title Insurance

Title insurance has evolved to become a vital element in most real estate transactions. Title insurance companies track all recorded documents and transfers of interests in real estate so they can issue *title insurance* — policies that assure the purchaser that the title to the property being transferred is legally valid and unblemished. This kind of title is commonly referred to as a *clean and marketable title.* Title insurance is like any form of insurance in that it defends and pays the claims made against the insured. Two types of title insurance policies are issued in most transactions:

- The seller provides one to the buyer to protect herself against claims that the purchase of the property wasn't a marketable title.

- Mortgage lenders require title insurance to protect against someone else claiming legal title to your property. The lender provides funds toward the purchase of the property and wouldn't be protected if the property ownership were to change based on a claim of an improper transfer of title.

Don't simply use the title insurance company that your real estate agent or lender suggests — shop around. Because many title companies provide escrow services, you need to watch out for companies that quote very low prices on one service and make up for it by overcharging in other areas. When you call around for title insurance and escrow fee quotes, get a handle on all the charges; there may be miscellaneous or hidden administrative fees that can sneak up on you and become major items — document preparation, notary services, courier fees, and express mail. If you find a company with lower prices, consider asking for an itemization in writing so you don't run into any surprises.

Property Insurance

You must have insurance, often one of the larger expenses for investment properties. Unless you purchase the property entirely for cash, you can't close the transaction and take over the property until you have a certificate of insurance in place. Your lender will prudently insist that you have adequate insurance coverage with policy limits that effectively protect your financer's collateral or financial interest in the property.

In accounting terms, property insurance is a *fixed expense* (like your property taxes), which means that although you may be able to turn off the natural gas (a *variable expense*) when your property is unoccupied, you must have insurance coverage — even if your property is vacant. In fact, insurance is more important if your property is vacant for an extended time frame.

To avoid surprises in your cash flow, determine the cost of insurance while you're still in your due diligence phase of the transaction. At this point, you retain the ability to cancel without penalty if you find that proper insurance coverage is either not available or priced out of your budget.

Another benefit of getting your insurance early in the due diligence process is that your insurance agent or an underwriter from the insurance company may inspect the property before providing you with a quote. Of course, any inspection by the insurance company is limited in scope and is never a substitute for your own inspection or the detailed written inspections you need from your property inspector (see Chapter 10). But it can be important to know whether the insurance company is going to require any upgrades or changes to the property as a condition of offering insurance.

You may trust your insurance broker or agent, but don't allow your escrow to close until you have written documentation confirming that your property insurance coverage is in force. It may seem improbable, but many properties have suffered a catastrophic loss or liability claim hours after the property changed hands and the new owner's insurance coverage wasn't yet in place.

Final Closing Statement

Just before your transaction is complete and escrow is closed, you receive a closing statement from the escrow officer. Besides the actual purchase price, several expenses are incurred in the process of purchasing real estate that must be worked out between the buyer and the seller. For example, the seller may have paid the property taxes for the balance of the year, and the buyer should reimburse him for the amount attributable to his ownership period after the close of escrow.

The buyer and seller need to pay some expenses, such as escrow and recording fees. Who pays what is usually outlined in the escrow instructions and is determined by a combination of the purchase agreement negotiations between the parties and custom and practice in the local real estate market. Table 11-1 contains a breakdown of the allocation of expenses that are typical in the purchase of investment properties.

Item	Paid by Seller	Paid by Buyer
Broker's commission	X	
Escrow fees	Split 50-50	Split 50-50
Recording fees: Loan payoff	X	
Recording fees: Transfer		X
Transfer tax	X	
State or local revenue stamps	X	
Seller's title policy	X	
Lender's title policy		X
Loan origination fee		X
Loan commitment fee		X
Appraisal		X
Credit report		X
Loan prepayment penalty, if any	X	

Table 11-1: *Typical Allocation of Expenses*

In addition to the allocation of expenses between the buyer and seller, the final closing statement contains *credits* (items that accrue to the benefit of the party receiving the credit) and *debits* (items that are paid out of escrow on behalf of the party being debited). Table 11-2 shows the usual accounting of the debits and credits on the closing or settlement statement.

Item	Buyer Credit	Buyer Debit	Seller Credit	Seller Debit	Prorated
Selling price		X	X		
Buyer's loan principal	X				
Buyer's loan points/fees		X			
Prepaid interest		X			
Property inspection fees/appraisal		X			
Payoff seller's loan				X	
Tenants' security deposits	X			X	
Buyer's earnest money deposit	X			X	
Additional cash down payment	X			X	
Unpaid bills (for example, utility charges)	X			X	X
Prepaid property taxes		X	X		X
Prepaid insurance		X	X		X
Prepaid expenses (for example, utility deposit)		X	X		X
Supplies left by seller for buyer's use		X	X		X

Table 11-2: *Usual Accounting on Closing Statement*

The day before you close on the property, take a brief walk-through to make sure everything is still in the condition it was before and that all the fixtures, appliances, window coverings, and other items the contract lists are still there. Sometimes, sellers ignore or don't recall these things and consequently don't leave what they agreed to in the sales contract.

The escrow officer or closing agent usually processes the mandatory reporting of the real estate transaction to the IRS and the state tax authorities, if required. If she doesn't file the required 1099-S form, the brokers or the buyer and seller may be required to handle the reporting, which includes the identity of the property transferred, the sales price, and the Social Security numbers of the buyer and seller.

Be sure to keep a copy of the closing statement because this document establishes your initial cost basis when you sell the property and need to determine your capital gain. Also, some of the expenses paid at the close of escrow may be deductible on your tax return, such as prepaid interest or points on your loan and property taxes and insurance.

Deed Recording and Property Takeover

Although the escrow officer may have all of the signed documents, and funds have been transferred to the proper accounts, you aren't the proud owner of your investment property until the deed is recorded. The procedure for recording the documents varies throughout the country but is becoming more standardized. Nearly every county uses a county recorder to record documents like real estate deeds, mortgages, deeds of trust, and other real estate documents as a public notice. Typically, there is an office of the county clerk and recorder, sometimes in the county courthouse in smaller jurisdictions.

Electronic document processing technology has made great strides in improving the efficiency in recording and retrieving documents at virtually all recorders' offices. Now documents can be retrieved by computers in a matter of seconds and are usually indexed by grantor and grantee.

After you receive word that the deed has been recorded, the transaction is finalized; you're the new owner, and you begin the property takeover process. You should take several steps in the first few days of ownership, including

- Conducting a final walk-through and inspection of both the property's exterior and interior to make sure the property hasn't been damaged before the close of escrow.

- Verifying that all items indicated on the personal property inventory list are present.

- Making sure all keys were received (if the property is vacant, you should change the locks as a precaution).

- Checking the utility meters to make sure the utility company has switched the billing as of the close of escrow so you don't get billed for the former owner's usage.

- Meeting with tenants and assuring them that you're a responsive and concerned property owner who wants to cooperatively resolve issues.

An issue to address right after the closing is the possession and control by the former owner. Because the escrow closing and recording can often happen during the day without any specific notice, it's best to wait until the following calendar day and personally verify that only the tenants that should be there are occupying the property. If the owner is still residing on the premises or is using some of the property for his own use, you need to immediately ask that he turn over full possession unless you've made other formal written arrangements in advance. To minimize this prospect, we suggest that you include significant daily monetary damages in the purchase contract for any unauthorized holdover usage by the seller.

Congratulations! You're now ready to begin managing your property and increasing its value as you build the foundation of your real estate portfolio.

_____

_____

_____

12

Selling Your Property

A successful investment strategy doesn't simply involve buying and operating properties. The *disposition* or *exit strategy* has a significant impact on overall success.

Begin your exit-strategy planning while you're acquiring property. That is, develop a game plan to work toward before you buy the asset. You can always change or modify your plans, but knowing your exit strategy before acquisition is good practice.

You do your homework, buy the right property at the right price, and add value by maintaining and improving the property and obtaining good tenants. So why undo your good work by selling the property for less than it's worth or paying too much in taxes because you failed to explore ways to defer your capital gains (which can keep more of your money working to keep your portfolio growing)?

When you're looking to buy rental real estate with appreciation potential, seek properties that have deferred maintenance and cosmetic problems that allow you to buy them at a good price. When you go to sell your property, you want to get full value, so before you list or show your property, scrutinize the curb appeal and physical condition, looking for those items that need attention. Don't rely on your own eye; ask a professional real estate agent or property manager who isn't familiar with the property to give you some feedback.

When it's time to sell the property, you have several options, but not all of them have the same tax consequences. We explain the most basic strategy — selling outright — in this chapter.

Sell Outright

One exit strategy is to simply sell the property and report the sale to the IRS. As long as capital gains tax rates are low, this strategy may work for taxpayers who are nearing the end of their prime real estate investing years and are looking to slow down and simplify their lives.

In an *outright* or *all-cash sale*, you simply sell the property, report the sale to the IRS, and determine whether you have a taxable gain or loss. If it's a gain, taxes are due; if you've held the property for at least 12 months, the low capital gains tax rates of 0 percent or 15 or 20 percent apply. Don't forget the 25 percent tax rate on cost recovery deduction that's triggered on the sale.

Although an outright or all-cash sale is fairly straightforward, real estate investors are often interested in postponing the recognition of their gain on sale so they can postpone the payment of taxes due. This situation is where an installment sale or an exchange can be useful.

Calculating Gain or Loss on a Sale

Preparing and retaining accurate records from the initial purchase of your rental property and throughout the ownership are extremely important because the sale of a real estate investment property must be reported to the IRS.

Several factors go into the required calculation to determine whether there's a gain or loss on the sale that can either increase or reduce the overall income:

- The sales price is a major factor.
- Any capital improvements made to the property should be included.
- Accumulated depreciation taken during the holding period increases your taxes when it's recaptured.
- If the property had operating losses that couldn't be taken in prior tax years, those suspended losses increase the adjusted basis and lower the potential taxable gain (or increase the loss available to shelter other income).

Table 12-1 outlines the following gain (or loss) on sale calculation.

Gross sales price	$1,500,000
Minus selling expenses	(50,000)
Net sales proceeds	1,450,000
Minus adjusted basis (see Table 12-2)	(700,000)
Total gain (or loss) on sale	$750,000

Table 12-1: *Calculating Total Gain or Loss on Sale*

Step 1: Determine the net sales proceeds

The *net sales proceeds* are the gross sales price minus the selling expenses. The *selling expenses* are all costs incurred to complete the sales transaction such as real estate commissions, attorney and accountant fees, settlement and escrow fees, title insurance, and other closing costs.

Step 2: Determine the adjusted basis for the property

When the property is just acquired, the *basis* is simply the original cost of the property (the equity down payment plus the total debt incurred to finance the property plus closing costs, appraisal, and environmental reports).

However, the basis isn't static — it changes during the ownership period. To adjust the original basis, take three factors into account (see Table 12-2 for the sample calculations):

Original acquisition cost or basis	$750,000
Plus capital improvements	50,000
Minus accumulated cost recovery	(100,000)
Minus any casualty losses taken	0
Adjusted basis	$700,000

Table 12-2: *Adjusted Basis Calculation*

- **Capital improvements:** During the holding period, owners often make some capital improvements or additions to the property. *Capital improvements* are money spent to improve the existing property or construct new property. These capital improvements are added to the original acquisition cost to determine the adjusted basis.

  Routine and normal repairs required to keep the property in good working order over its useful life are deductible expenses during the tax year in which they're incurred. They're not capital improvements for the purpose of the adjusted basis calculation. A capital improvement includes all costs incurred such as contractor payments, architect fees, building permits, construction materials, and labor costs.

- **Depreciation:** The straight-line depreciation taken each tax year is accumulated and reduces the adjusted basis of the property. Note that the total accumulated depreciation is included in the overall calculation of the gain or loss upon sale as part of the adjusted basis but is reported separately and is taxed at a different rate on the taxpayer's tax return.

- **Casualty losses taken by the taxpayer:** Casualty losses can result from the destruction of or damage to your property from any sort of sudden, unexpected, or unusual event.

Step 3: Determine the total gain or loss on the sale

The total gain or loss is determined by taking the net sales price and subtracting the adjusted basis (see Table 12-1).

Step 4: Factor in accumulated cost recovery and suspended losses

If you have suspended losses reported on the taxpayer's tax returns during the ownership period, deduct them from the net sales proceeds (see Table 12-3). The *suspended losses* are those losses that the taxpayer couldn't use in prior tax years because he didn't meet the strict IRS requirements. That figure is the *capital gain from appreciation.*

_____

_____

_____

Total gain on sale (from Table 12-1)	$750,000
Minus straight-line cost recovery	(100,000)
Minus suspended losses	(75,000)
Capital gain from appreciation	$575,000

Table 12-3: *Capital Gain from Appreciation*

Step 5: Determine total tax liability

The net gain on sale is taxed as ordinary income unless the property was held for more than twelve months. Fortunately, most real estate investors hold the property for more than twelve months and can qualify for the lower long-term capital gains tax rates. In fact, if the property has been held less than twelve months, all depreciation that has been taken is recaptured as ordinary income.

For tax purposes, the net gain on sale must be allocated between the capital gain from appreciation and the recapture of the accumulated depreciation. The seller doesn't automatically get the benefits of the lower flat 0 or 15 percent maximum capital gains tax and may even have to pay the maximum depreciation recapture tax rate of 25 percent if she's in a higher income tax bracket. (The depreciation recapture rate is based on your ordinary income tax bracket but won't exceed 25 percent.)

In Table 12-3, the total gain on sale of $750,000 is reduced by $100,000 in accumulated depreciation and suspended losses of $75,000 for a gain from appreciation of $575,000. In Table 12-4, we break the taxation of the capital gain down between capital gain from appreciation and depreciation recapture. The accumulated depreciation is recaptured at 25 percent, resulting in a tax liability of $25,000. The gain from appreciation was taxed at the maximum capital gains flat rate of 20 percent, resulting in a tax liability of $115,000. So the total tax liability is $140,000.

Straight-line cost recovery	$100,000
Times tax rate on recapture	25%
Total tax due for recapture	$25,000
Capital gain from appreciation	$575,000
Times tax rate on capital gain	20%
Total tax due on capital gain	$115,000
Total tax liability	$140,000

Table 12-4: *Total Tax Liability Calculation*

If the sale of the property results in a net loss, the loss must first be applied to offset net passive-activity income or gains. If there are none, or after they're exhausted, the net loss can be applied to reduce the income or gains from nonpassive activities such as earned income or wages.

About the Authors

Eric Tyson, MBA, is a best-selling author and syndicated columnist. Through his counseling, writing, and teaching, he equips people to manage their personal finances better and successfully direct their investments. Eric is a former management consultant to Fortune 500 financial service firms and has successfully invested in real estate for more than three decades.

Robert S. Griswold, MSBA, is a successful real estate investor and active, hands-on property manager with a large portfolio of residential and commercial rental properties who uses print and broadcast journalism to bring his many years of experience to his readers, listeners, and viewers.